The Common Angler

A CELEBRATION

OF FISHING

The Common Angler

A CELEBRATION OF FISHING

Jack Wollitz

Cover & inside photos by Jack Wollitz
Front & back covers designed by Lee-Ann Mitchell DeMeo
Edited by David Bushman
Book designed by Scott Ryan

Published in the USA by Fayetteville Mafia Press
Columbus, Ohio

Contact Information
Email: fayettevillemafiapress@gmail.com
Website: fayettevillemafiapress.com

ISBN: 9781949024227
eBook ISBN: 9781949024234

DEDICATION

We who go to the water to fish have three things in common. Maybe more, but at our core, we think, we enjoy, and we are passionate. This book is for all who compose the community commonly known as "anglers." It is a huge community, its population far too large to occupy any city on our Earth. I am fortunate to have come to know many who call themselves anglers. The way in which they go about their fishing business helped me grow as a fisher and as a person.

This book is dedicated to all whose fishing time and experiences I have been fortunate to have enjoyed. If you have been in my boat or I have been in yours, if you have stood by my side in a river or on a beach, or joined me on a pier, dam, or causeway, you have inspired this book. If you have tapped out an article or social media post or made a TV show that caught my attention, you are a reason I have written this book.

Finally, I dedicate *The Common Angler* to two people without whom I might be somebody else altogether. My father, Robert, took me to the water when I was very young and delivered the bricks and mortar for my fishing foundation. Wife Barb provides support, encouragement, understanding, and, when needed, consolation. She has been a fishing companion, but, to her credit, on terms that do not include predawn launches or cold, rainy weather. Most of all, of course, she provides love.

To them and to all the others, thank you for shaping my world of fishing.

CONTENTS

Preface...1

Chapter 1: An angler is born...4

Chapter 2: The passion that smolders 7

Chapter 3: Why is there water?...10

Chapter 4: Why are there fish?..12

Chapter 5: Fishing with friends..14

Chapter 6: This is for the birds...18

Chapter 7: Chubs and suckers..21

Chapter 8: Expedition to Weller's Pond................................24

Chapter 9: Game fish in the eye of the beholder...................27

Chapter 10: Fishing in our complicated world......................30

Chapter 11: Coping with the coronavirus..............................32

Chapter 12: Me, myself, and I..35

Chapter 13: In a word . . . say what?......................................38

Chapter 14: If docks could talk..41

Chapter 15: The most worrisome snag of all time.................45

Chapter 16: You gotta hold your mouth just right.................49

Chapter 17: She's my boat..52

Chapter 18: Eat, breathe, fish...57

Chapter 19: Mine's bigger than yours....................................60

Chapter 20: A little more salt, please 64

Chapter 21: When the story must be told.................................70

Chapter 22: An angler of mythical proportions.................73

Chapter 23: Hemingway, Williams, and Boggs.................77

Chapter 24: When anglers finds his mission.................80

Chapter 25: On the water with big game hunters 84

Chapter 26: A wizard in walleye world.................88

Chapter 27: My favorite place to fish.................92

Chapter 28: Greeting the sun.................96

Chapter 29: Bump in the night.................99

Chapter 30: What would Izaak Walton say?.................102

Chapter 31: Waist-deep in ice water (and other things to fear).................106

Chapter 32: That Erie feeling.................110

Chapter 33: A spectacularly disappointing three seconds.................114

Chapter 34: Ouch! That's going to hurt.................117

Chapter 35: When it hurts, go fishing.................120

Chapter 36: 'Interesting' is not a euphemism.................122

Chapter 37: To stink or not to stink.................124

Chapter 38: Alligators and bouncing bobbers.................127

Chapter 39: That's Hollywood.................130

Chapter 40: The angler's obligation.................133

Chapter 41: Red tide and caring voices.................137

Final words: Where we've been and where we're going.................141

Acknowledgments.................144

Preface

The world needs people who are happy to share their passions. Fishing is my passion, or, to keep the peace among family and friends, *one* of my passions. Writing is another.

It is a privilege to write about fishing. I am neither the best fisherman nor the best writer. Nor am I the best fishing writer. But I have had audiences for more than forty years who have read what I write, so I forge on.

Perhaps I've inspired some people to fish. I don't know for sure. Nobody has ever told me they took up fishing because they read what I've written. I suspect some have, but I cannot prove that.

I do know, however, that people enjoy reading about fishing. That's why I have written about it for two-thirds of my life. I am motivated by the wonderful opportunity to share my passion about fishing and provide enjoyment for those who like to read about the things that make fishing interesting. I also know that everybody has a story worth telling and that many interesting stories lurk among seemingly common, ordinary events and circumstances. I enjoy finding those stories and sharing them. That is the simple reason behind the forty-two essays in this collection.

It is good to be passionate about things. It's good to be passionate about your family, your friends, your country, your interests—whatever captures your fancy.

This book is for those who are passionate about things. You know your passions and how valuable they are in providing context and meaning to your very existence. When we recognize our passions, we gain reasons to enjoy life and living. Passions, I believe, are metaphors. They are real in and of themselves, but actually represent something far more significant to their owners than merely the acts of fishing or golfing, making music or painting pictures, collecting automobiles or working with wood.

Metaphorically speaking, you may be swimming in interests other than those in which I swim. But we are connected by the fact that we are passionate about life and living. I would imagine a person who is passionate about cooking or carving, hiking or haikus would still find the stories on these pages interesting.

Water is another subject about which many are passionate. Water pulls us. Watching water soothes us as we gaze in wonder at what life resides under the surface of the ocean, the lake, the river, or the puddle.

It's no wonder we are attracted to water. It is the wellspring of life, composed of two of the elements essential for carbon-based life forms. That Earth has water is one of the facts that make our planet special. We have a primordial attraction to water, a DNA link we share with long-extinct species scientists say wiggled their way to dry land to start a new colony for creatures that would rather crawl than swim.

Perhaps my own fascination with water is the reason I love to fish. My interest in fishing dates to an exact day I can no longer remember. But it certainly was an important moment, the day when something in my brain clicked and said, "That was fun. Let's do it again."

And so it has been. I've fished again and again and again. I have spent more days on the water than I could ever count. Along the way, fishing became a passion, a way of life for a man who has been blessed to have persevered through bitter cold and stifling heat, through utter failure and amazing success, through pain and pleasure, even through ridicule and accolade.

Like many things that deserve passionate pursuit, fishing is not a finite experience. Try as we might, no angler will ever achieve ultimate success. Rather, fishermen and fisherwomen set personal goals for a day or a week or a lifetime that are based not so much on what they catch as on the level of satisfaction they can wring from each experience.

This reminds me of a story told to a group of fishing writers by bass fishing impresario Ray Scott. He founded the Bass Anglers Sportsman Society, and made millions of dollars through developing ways to touch the emotions of avid anglers. Scott told us writers about a BASS member who died and went to Heaven, where the greeting angel introduced the departed angler to his eternal dream: he would fish every day on a lake so bass filled that he would catch a fish on every cast.

It was beyond the angler's wildest dreams. He loved his first day in Heaven, and naturally he ventured out at daybreak and caught a big bass on his very first cast. The next cast and hundreds more that day all produced the same result—a jarring strike and a line-stretching battle. No fish spit the hook. The line never broke. No cast went ignored.

Day two in Heaven was a carbon copy of day one. Ditto for day three. By the end of his first week in his afterlife, the poor soul came to recognize his ultimate destination might not be Heaven after all.

I love fishing because I never know exactly what will happen when I push the boat from the dock and head out across the water. It's what makes it worthy of passion. I'm pleased to share some of my favorite experiences and observations with hope they will draw a smile on your face, touch a nerve you didn't know you had, or simply serve to justify what you've known all along.

And that is that fishing is a passion and that anglers are among the most fortunate people on our watery planet. Now let's celebrate those who share the passion.

Jack Wollitz
May 2021

CHAPTER 1

An angler is born

Three-quarters of Earth is covered with water. Considering that fact, I am not surprised fishing interests and intrigues so many people.

My fascination with fishing goes back to a fuzzy beginning. Such also is the case for the human species' connection to water, fish, and fishing. We cannot pinpoint the defining moment when a man or a woman caught a fish and gained a sense of accomplishment. But it's certain such moments happened.

I do not remember the first fish I caught. I do, however, recall two very early fishing experiences.

One involves an inky-black night and clinging humidity, a hissing green Coleman lantern hanging over the side of a leaky aluminum boat. I sat midship, my father at the stern and an uncle at the bow. Insects fluttered around the glaring light, some falling to the water after venturing too close to the heat. Little fish swarmed in the glow that penetrated just under the lake's surface.

The elders in the boat knew crappies and white bass would be attracted to the baitfish eating the bugs. Dad and Uncle Bill hung their baits in the vicinity, and happily reeled in the panfish they had tricked.

Another experience was a daytime adventure to a quarry pond, the perimeter of which was lined with big rocks. Hordes of bluegills hovered around the boulders to hide from bigger predators while feasting on the life that crawled out of the crevices.

I remember lobbing small hooks baited with garden worms to the colorful bluegills. The line was black, probably Dacron or some other synthetic fiber woven into a thin braid. But the bluegills didn't notice. They attacked the baited hooks ravenously.

Those two experiences are on the distant edge of my angling memory. I can still see the scenes, but details—like whether I caught anything—have faded. I can only suspect that I must have had some kind of success, in whatever measure that might have been, because I jumped at every chance to return to the water.

One day, not too many years after those earliest experiences, I was out again with my father at the sportsman's club where he was a member. The club grounds included a deep, clear, weed-rimmed lake that had been created by coal strip miners many years previous. Dad was shooting on the rifle range. But I had one thought in mind whenever I went to his club: go fishing in that pond.

On this particular day, the clouds were big and puffy against the deep blue sky. A westerly breeze blew seeds from the weeds across the scruffy landscape, and big gray grasshoppers flitted out in front of me as I flushed them on my lope to the lake. In one hand, I clutched a bouncy spinning rod with an ancient Pflueger Supreme reel spooled with fishing line of questionable vintage.

A moment of inspiration prompted me to grab a few of the hoppers. They squirmed and scratched in my hand and excreted "tobacco juice" on my palm. So I decided to cram them into my pocket—a lousy bait container, for sure, and one that was not particularly conducive to keeping my grasshoppers in tip-top condition.

As I cleared the last rise and scanned the crystal water before me, I spied a solitary largemouth bass finning lazily between the bank and the inner edge of the weed line that rimmed the lake. Instinct told me to approach the water with stealth.

Finally in position to make an offering to the cruising bass, I fumbled around in my pocket and pulled out a somewhat injured grasshopper. Its body was big enough to hold up to my efforts to hook it to my line, and I tossed the bait a few feet from the bass. The fish immediately darted out of sight.

I left the bait out on the water, where it struggled to take flight. The buzzing wings created a tight series of concentric circles. Soon enough, the bass reappeared and hovered just under the surface, below the insect. The buzzing stopped and the fish lost interest. But in one more effort to lift itself off the lake, the grasshopper sent out another thrashing message: vulnerable creature available for the taking.

It was like a neon sign to the lurking largemouth.

The bass lunged up and took the bait in a poetry-in-motion swirl. I jerked, the fish dove, and the battle was on with what was up to that point the biggest fish I'd ever seen, much less hooked. Some say largemouths are lazy fighters, but not this fish. It leaped from the water, shook its head, and showered the surface with thousands of droplets. It belly flopped back into the lake and churned in an effort to free itself.

My line held, and the hook stayed stuck. As I dragged the bass toward the mud at my feet, I gained a sense of accomplishment that I'd never felt before. And as I freed the bass, I knew I wanted to do that again. And again and again.

And so, this angler was born.

Jack Wollitz learned early about the thrill of fishing.

CHAPTER 2

The passion that smolders

Fifty and more years have passed since my first encounter with a fish bigger than my hand. While that initial catch is forever etched in my mind, untold numbers of other catches somehow have eluded memory.

I would guess that would be the case for the multitude of zealous fishers around our world. We remember the highlights—the first, the biggest, the weirdest, and other extremes—but the routine catches have faded into the blur of history.

This is not to say we have grown weary of the fishing experience. For all of us who call ourselves anglers, some distant catch flinted a spark, a flicker of heat that fell on a place in our souls where it could smolder until the next cast, the next catch, the next trip to the water.

All of us who fish share that smoldering ember. It is our common denominator. It was lit by an experience too good to dismiss. It stays warm because we have the perfect place to keep it in our soul. And it fans to flames every time the water calls.

And the water called one blustery autumn Saturday several years ago.

It was Halloween, actually, and October 31 is not the best day of the year to go bass fishing in Ohio. Where I live, the last day of October can be seventy-five degrees or thirty. Sunny or snowy. But it's never the best of all days to cast for bass.

Nevertheless, we went to the lake. A front was pushing across the region, propelling rain clouds with a 20 mph wind that gusted to thirty, and the day's high temperature had already been reached when we launched my boat shortly after first light. My friend Steve Zarbaugh and I laughed at our foolish expectations of catching anything of consequence.

The water temperature was fifty-three degrees following a nice stretch of sunny and mild days. That was good news, we calculated, since two weeks earlier we'd fished with success in forty-nine-degree water. A few degrees of warming can be a big deal to autumn bass.

Our optimism cooled as the thermometer dropped. The wind gusted under a swirling gray sky, and raindrops pelted my glasses. Our hands were cold, and the three small bass that bit during the first couple of hours on the water did nothing to warm them up.

But then my friend struck his jig into the jaw of a fine smallmouth bass. It bulldogged under the boat for a moment and made a showy jump off the starboard side. The smallie weighed three pounds, ten ounces and fanned the fires in both of us fishermen, warming us up for another hour on the water.

Fifteen minutes later, I noticed the slightest bit of resistance as I dragged my jig down a rocky ledge that stairstepped from ten feet down to twenty-five. I eased the rod tip up and felt a sign of life on the business end of my fluorocarbon line. It twitched as the fish tugged, so I jerked and was rewarded with the sensation that all anglers covet. The rod loaded into a big, bucking arc and pulled the weight of the fish a foot or so off the bottom.

A hookset that hauls only water is all too familiar to all of us who fish. We cannot even begin to guess how many times we have struck back at a suspected "bite" and failed to connect. Was it a fish? A twig? Or did our senses trick us altogether?

Wise anglers quickly come to realize that hooksets are free, so whenever there's a doubt, we jerk.

I gained ground on the churning fish, and as smallmouths typically do, this one charged to the top. It surfaced around the midsection of my boat and zoomed to my right, narrowly missing dragging the line along the shaft of the trolling motor dangling off the bow.

My eyes bugged wide as I spied the size of the fish. It was big and bronze, and now it was threatening to escape. I wanted the fish in my hands, even though I would release it, as my reward for a long day of patience and endurance.

The smallie tired soon enough and I pulled it from the water. Using the thumb-in-the-mouth grip that all bass fishers employ, I quieted the flopping fish and popped the jig from the roof of its mouth. Big smallmouths tend to get fleshy around their faces, and this one had lots of muscle around its jaws.

It weighed four pounds on the nose. Good enough to beat my buddy's bronzeback. And certainly good enough to fan the embers in my soul to burn my fishing fever over the long winter months that would follow this special Halloween treat.

Catches like this sparked the author's
passion for fishing.

CHAPTER 3

Why is there water?

You might guess the answer to my question "Why is there water?"

It's for the fish.

Yes, of course water is essential for life on Earth. Water means so much to us earthlings that if it were to be siphoned off our planet, we'd pretty much be extinct in a matter of days.

But as a fisherman, I am forever grateful that water is where the fish live. Because fish live in water, I am inclined to frequent watery places.

For more than half of my life, my favorite water has been where bass live. Whether largemouth, smallmouth, or spotted, bass today occupy the uppermost spot on my list of favorite game fish. I love acres of lily pads, miles of reeds and cattails, and lush patches of coontail, milfoil, and hydrilla. Drop a treetop, a brush pile, or a point dotted with flooded willows into the mix and I'm in bass heaven. Give me a sharp drop or a big rock off a Lake Erie flat and I'm for sure betting a school of big smallies is down there looking for the lure I'm going to drop into its midst.

This is not to say I pass up opportunities on other water.

I have awakened at dawn during beach vacations and stood first in line at the bait store with money in hand to buy enough shrimp or bloodworms to get me through a morning of casting for croakers, speckled trout, redfish, or striped bass.

I will drive two hours in the wee hours of the morning to a streamside parking spot, pull on waders, and string up a rod with a tiny nymph to drift past the noses of ten-pound steelhead.

I'll forgo an afternoon of great football on TV to scrabble along the rocks of a break wall or causeway in search of one more autumn haul of crappies or bluegills before my local lakes freeze over.

It is the water that attracts me, providing me with the opportunity to satisfy some primordial urge to discover what I cannot readily see. It's a frontier that I never grow weary of exploring. I may have caught ten thousand fish; I don't know because I've never counted them, though it does seem like a reasonable guess. But I cannot resist the challenge of catching number 10,001.

Sometimes I wonder what I would do if I did not fish. I guess I would still go to the water. Probably. I might swim. I might kayak. I might even try paddleboarding. It looks interesting. Or I might just do what many do and gaze at its ever-changing vista. No two moments are the same on the water.

Water is where life began. And for me, water is where life takes on additional meaning.

Like the deer that must swim to the other side of the river,
we are attracted to the water by a primordial urge to
discover what is under the surface.

CHAPTER 4

Why are there fish?

Our planet is a maze of ecosystems—from desert to forest, from prairie to suburban yard, from mountain to valley, and all of the other places on Earth. They all, regardless of location, require water to function as life-sustaining systems.

Our oceans, rivers, and lakes are places where a special form of life developed. They are home to the world's fish—so numerous and diverse that even today new species are being discovered.

No matter your personal belief about the establishment of life on Earth, it is clear the plants and animals are pretty well equipped for the niches they occupy. People need all manner of special gear to survive immersed. And a fish out of water is doomed if not returned within a minute or two.

Like every species of flora and fauna, fish are part of the Earth's food chain. Individual varieties rank at different levels in that chain, but the fact is a fish lives in an eat-and-be-eaten world.

Fish have been eating each other for millions of years. For probably a similar number of years, certain land animals—mammals, birds, and reptiles among them—ventured into the water to catch and eat fish. It was all in a day's work in the eat-and-be-eaten world, and fish were a cornerstone of the nutritional foundation.

It is this fact that brings us to the current place in time. Humans learned to do what other animals were doing. A heron might not learn anything about fishing from an otter, but humans certainly could take a lesson or two from both species.

Fish are food. They often live within a spear jab from dry land. And they are abundant enough that schools of fish sometimes can be corralled, grabbed by hand, and tossed to the bank, the same banks where the earliest shore-lunch cooks were waiting.

Fish were there to be eaten. People were there to eat. It was a match made in heaven.

In prehistoric fishing cultures, the best fishermen were the healthiest. They ate when there were no fruits to pick, no deer to slaughter. Even today, cultures with diets tilted toward fish experience fewer problems with heart disease and cancers. When I was a little boy, my family convinced me fish was "brain food," so I imagined myself better equipped for tomorrow's arithmetic test after eating oven-heated fish sticks and Mom's salmon patties.

That little bit of recollection is a hint of how impressionable I was in my schoolboy days. Here's another: my grandfather once counseled me that if I spit on my bait, I'd catch more fish. So you know where this story is heading.

It was a hot and humid summer night. Dad and I were fishing with family elders during an overnight campout at a reservoir near our home in Youngstown, Ohio. I do not recall much about that evening save for two things: it was very muggy, and Grandpa revealed his secrets about spitting on the bait.

I was too young to be entrusted with casting, especially in the darkness, so I had no bait personally to spike with spit. But I busied myself as Dad, Grandpa, and the uncles prepared to lob another gob of night crawlers to the catfish we hoped to catch. I no doubt worked myself into a pretty good sweat bobbing from one pole to the next.

Like I said, I don't recall much about that trip, including the results of the fishing, but I am guessing I slept well when we finally retired to our cots at the campsite. Spitting on all those hooks is pretty tiring work. It's a lot of responsibility for a young fellow.

So to answer my "Why are there fish?" question further, I believe we have fish so youngsters can learn all the secrets their elders care to share. I cannot imagine growing up without fish stories like the ones I experienced.

CHAPTER 5
Fishing with friends

Many, many years ago, two couples hopped in a Chevy van to which a fifteen-foot runabout's trailer was attached. The little boat was no doubt a bit on the small side for four adults, especially considering one of them was eight months pregnant.

But we were determined to spend the day fishing for perch and rock bass around the boulders and riprap that rimmed the harbor of Ashtabula, a little town on Ohio's Lake Erie coastline. Word had filtered that the panfish were biting. News like that makes sensible people forget about little details like boat capacity and birthing babies.

And so we drove merrily to the lake. It was May, and who cannot help but be merry in May?

As it turned out, our trip was productive. We caught enough fish to feed two families for a day or so. But better than that, we had more fun than we might have imagined. The trip transcended simply being the means to get fillets for the skillet. We laughed. We told stories. We made up names for the fish we caught and even tried to keep score to determine whether the guys or the girls were better anglers on that particular day.

Soon enough, we lost count, but it didn't really matter. We cast care to the wind. We ate ham and cheese sandwiches and M&M's candy, guzzled Cokes and Mountain Dews. We basked in the mild weather and reeled in fish all day. We had a contingency plan in case the baby decided it was her birthday, but fortunately for us, we didn't need to activate it. Fun was the order of the day.

Left: Retired Major League Baseball umpire John Hirschbeck with a bass caught while fishing with author Jack Wollitz. Right: Rich Getch and a big bass he boated while fishing with golf buddy Jack Wollitz.

And so it has been on a thousand fishing trips ever since. Many, I am happy to say, have been with the best people I know.

Fishing and friends go together like peanut butter and jelly. Both are good by themselves, but when you put them together, it's a pretty special treat.

In the spirit of full disclosure, I like to fish solo. I write about that later in this book. But when the opportunity to take a friend fishing arises, I'm the first to say, "Let's go!"

Wife Barb and friends Jolane and Gary Day were the coconspirators in that friends' fishing trip. Over the years, I've had the great pleasure to share the ups and downs of many days on the boat with perhaps a hundred others. As though the trips were yesterday, the memories are legion, and with each name I see a face: Several Daves; five Bobs; a couple Bruces, Rons, Jeffs, Jims, Larrys, Mikes, Marks, and Steves; another Jack; a Carmen, Charlie, Dale, Dan, Max, Micky, Ricky, Rick, Rich, Nick, Jo, Joe, Jason, John, Ted, Tim, Todd, Tom, Tony, Tyler, Gary, Kevin, Guido, Dion, George, Bill, Will, Rosie, Harry, Pat, Glenn, and even a D'Arcy; a Wendy; and a Jill. The list could be even more extensive if I applied myself.

And of course, wife Barb and daughter Betsy are on the list too.

If you pressed me, I could come up with a fact or two from just about any specific fishing trip with friends or family.

It is not difficult, for example, to remember fun excursions with Barb and Betsy. Like many mothers and daughters, they had a bit of a competitive streak between them. More golfer than fisherwoman, Barb loved playing miniature golf with Betsy when she was old enough to be a legitimate opponent. They dueled around local minigolf courses like Arnold Palmer and Jack Nicklaus. Neither was willing to concede.

Their competitiveness spilled out onto the lake. On lazy summer afternoons, we enjoyed anchoring in the shade of a highway bridge near our home to fish for bluegills and crappies. We could count on finding panfish galore feeding around the bridge's steel pilings. Speeding automobiles and heavy semitrucks rumbled overhead, and the clickety-clack of tires traversing padded gaps between the concrete slabs set the afternoons' cadence.

Fish that live in environments like that become conditioned to the constant noise. Anglers, on the other hand, must speak loudly to be heard as they fish under a highway bridge. Voices also become louder in the heat of battle.

Soon after we discovered the highway panfish action, the girls learned they could needle each other by keeping score.

"That's nine for me and seven for you."

"No way. I caught ten."

"This one's the biggest yet."

"Huh! Not even close to the one I caught."

And so it went. I was the bait man. I also had the unhooking duties. If

I was even a few seconds slow in threading a new bit of bait on one of the girls' jigs, I was scolded. The competition was always catch and release because Betsy considered it bad form to kill our catch, so I was careful with deeply hooked fish. But that also meant I might have her jig out of action for a few minutes while Mom was catching up.

There was no prize other than perhaps cookies and Cokes. But the girls fished as hard as tournament anglers casting for a king's ransom. They whipped casts back to the fish waiting in the piling shadows and reeled in catches at breakneck speed.

Amazingly, no one was hooked during those summer afternoon mom-and-daughter panfish derbies. But even though no blood was spilled, one of them might feign hurt feelings.

Anything, I assumed, to gain a leg up on the other.

The author's daughter, Betsy, competed with Mom in panfish-catching derbies as Dad baited their hooks and freed their catches.

CHAPTER 6
This is for the birds

From the haven where I am writing this, I have a panoramic view. An osprey is working with graceful diligence over a series of ponds known to hold nice populations of largemouth bass, tilapia, and cichlids. It is riding the morning thermals, banking on the breeze with neck tilted at just the right angle for sharp eyes to detect evidence of fish near the water's surface within reach of the raptor's sharp talons.

While I have been watching, the fishing osprey has made several passes over the nearest pond, circling in sweeping arcs and pausing on fluttering wings that feather the breeze long enough to permit more thorough scrutiny of the water below. I have been watching for thirty minutes, but so far the osprey's efforts have not resulted in a fish catch.

Reminds me of most of our fishing trips.

Birds have long been inspiration for anglers. We learned long ago that the best clues to the presence of game fish are the birds that stalk the shore and glide overhead. Like human anglers, fishing birds do not always connect. But unlike human anglers, they must catch or they will starve.

Herons and egrets simply do not bother to fish barren banks. They step high and lightly to gain advantageous positions from which they can rocket their beaks to grab small fish, frogs, and snakes, all of which are equally sought after by bass, pike, muskies, and other freshwater predator fish.

Gulls and terns join the fray out on the open water when schools of baitfish are pushed to the surface by marauding predators. They dive like air-to-surface missiles when the bait is thrashing, signaling no doubt to nearby anglers that fish worth catching are up and active.

Raptors' eyesight is their tactical advantage as they fish their way to success and sustenance. Ospreys and eagles are the killer aircraft in nature's battle for survival, delivering death blows from high above the water's surface.

The cormorant, loon, and anhinga are more like otters and seals than birds as they dive to snatch fish hiding far below the reach of raptors' talons.

And then there are pelicans. Watching them fish proves brute force is mighty effective. While eagles take finesse to high levels, pelicans are more like bowling balls dropping from the sky, with mouths agape to gulp fish that certainly die wondering what exactly hit them.

So, we see birds are pretty good at fishing. They must be, of course, or they will die. They know where and when to fish, scoring daily with a much higher batting average than human anglers. Interestingly, however, birds are nature's proof there are many ways to catch fish. They stalk on land, water, and air, all senses keyed to detect motion and life. Some strike with missile swiftness. Some employ submarine warfare. Others dive-bomb from the heights. All are effective. For that reason, it is wise to take a few pointers from our feathered friends.

Barb and I watched in awe one day on a lake near home as an adult bald eagle swooped low over the tree line on a dive toward the lake just one hundred yards from our boat. The magnificent bird zeroed in on a target point and pushed its talons forward at the critical moment. Its feet skimmed the surface, and then the eagle hit the afterburners to gain altitude and bank back to the trees. At first glance, we thought it had failed because its talons grabbed only water.

Less than a minute later, a juvenile eagle duplicated the flight pattern and tilted down to the water, where its talons skimmed the surface for a foot or two before it also rose and glided back to the woods. The two birds continued the routine two more times.

We were fortunate to witness an adult eagle teaching its offspring to fish. Amazing. It was like we had a real-world seat in a TV nature documentary.

Today when I fish, I look for the birds. Diving gulls, stalking shorebirds, plunging pelicans, submarining cormorants, and soaring raptors all are nature's way of saying, "Fish here." It's not exactly a neon arrow flashing to the target, but it is a sign as sure as any that conditions are right and the fish are there to be caught.

Anglers can learn a lot from watching how birds catch fish.

CHAPTER 7
Chubs and suckers

This never occurred to me until later in my life, but the idyllic days of my youth spent fishing for chubs and suckers were the foundation of the approach I have applied in preparing for and executing today on the water.

Looking back, I can see the bricks and mortar. They took shape during dewy summer mornings when I dragged a shovel to the family garden to turn over moist dirt in search of worms to drop into the empty tin-plated steel can I rescued from the family trash. I liberated empty Campbell's or Green Giant cans to lug bait to Yellow Creek where it traipsed close to my neighborhood's boundary with the municipal forest in the village of Poland, Ohio.

Bait collected, I bicycled to friends' houses with my fishing rod secured under my thumbs across the handlebars. Together we fishing buddies coasted down the street to the stream. I'm pretty certain the line on my reel was at least as old as I was; I had not yet learned about such angling preparedness lessons as the value of changing line to avoid the heartache of tangles and, worse, break-offs.

But I'm also pretty sure the hook was rightsized for the tiny mouths of the chubs and suckers we expected to catch. Experience dictated the amount of split shot needed to get the bait down in the gentle current and the precise depth to set the bobber for the perfect drift in the deeper pools of Yellow Creek, where the hungry fish were waiting. They seem now like little and obvious decisions, but they all contributed to learning.

Life is all about learning. And so it goes with fishing.

I was reminded of the advance work recently as I busied myself the day before a bass tournament with the chore of rigging rods for competition. Just as proper preparedness saved precious fishing time for me when I was ten, all of those carefully tied knots and smartly selected lures would be ready to serve when called on during the tournament. In pays to be organized in a boat laden with fifteen rod and reel combinations and more than one hundred pounds of soft plastics, jigs, crankbaits, spinnerbaits, buzzbaits, topwater lures, hooks, sinkers, extra spools of line, clippers, pliers, and other tools and gadgets. To put that in perspective, imagine that today I take as much weight of lures to the lake as I weighed when I was ten years old.

Pretournament prep time today typically is sixty minutes, but I can stretch it to two hours when I'm in a tinkering mood. The tinkering thing has deep roots. Dad was a tool and die maker who could machine a piece of steel into an unimaginably complicated gadget that enabled production-line workers to fashion signal transmission systems for General Motors automobiles. He also is a skilled model maker who even well into his nineties builds scale-model warplanes that look real enough to fly off the table.

I did not inherit much of Dad's talent for detail and precision. In fact, very little skill trickled from my fingers when I attempted to glue together the pieces and parts of Revell racing cars and airplanes. But I did have the inspiration to try; eventually I discovered I could whittle away on a length of pine cut from an old broomstick and reach the point where it resembled the manufactured lures I'd seen on store shelves. I created a popping plug, a shallow-running crankbait with a diving bill fashioned from plastic cut from a cottage cheese tub, and a minnow plug resembling (in shape, not in quality) the Rapala lures that were gaining popularity in those days.

With a little tinkering and tweaking, I eventually reached the point where I felt they might actually catch a fish. I keep them in my workshop to this day as a reminder of the time when my dreams were beginning to take form and substance.

All of the experiences digging worms, selecting hooks and sinkers, learning to read the water for eddies and current breaks, casting and retrieving without too much line twist, and experimenting with making and testing artificial lures served a very important role in my angling upbringing.

I learned what worked and what didn't. I gained the foundation on which even today I continue to stack new lessons and new successes. My early bricks and mortar today support a skyscraper.

Making it all possible were the chubs and suckers in the little creek near our house.

Frankly, catching chubs and suckers can easily be taken for granted. They were there to be taken without a whole bunch of effort. When the right bit of worm drifts within their vicinity, chubs and suckers aren't shy about eating the bait. I learned how to distinguish between bumping bottom and the bite of a fish. I learned how to deliver the cast in the seam of the current so that the hook with the worm would wash toward the waiting quarry. I learned when to adjust as the water rose or fell and when the sun pushed across the sky to cast shadows over new hiding holes.

Indeed, I had taken chubs and suckers for granted. But one day a coworker helped me regain appreciation for the importance they had in my life of fishing. It had been many decades since I last floated worms for them when coworker Doug and I were talking about the things we did when we were kids. He grew up fifty miles from where I did, but we'd both fished little streams during the long hot summers of our youth.

For him, Doug said, it was all about "fishing for chubs and suckers."

His words hit me smack across the forehead. "Chubs and suckers." Such a poetic phrase, really. Say it with an exclamation point. "Chubs and suckers!" Or say it with a simple period. "Chubs and suckers." Or say it with an ellipsis. "Chubs and suckers . . . "

I can say it in jubilation, as a matter of fact, or with a wisp of nostalgia, but "chubs and suckers" are no doubt the cornerstone of my own fishing foundation and almost certainly critical in many, if not most, other anglers' formative years. Chubs and suckers have helped make many a common angler.

Expedition to Weller's Pond

Yellow Creek was a good enough fishery for my friends and me when we were ten or eleven years old. We scratched our fishing itch often there, leaving our footprints in the same soft mud where Native Americans had left theirs, in the primordial forest near the subdivision where our parents lived.

But like the ancient anglers, we yearned for fishier waters around the next bend, over the hills, where bigger streams flowed, or in the pages of *Outdoor Life* and *Field & Stream*. We yearned for any place where adventure awaited those fortunate to gain access.

For some, that adventure is on a tributary of the Amazon, deep in a rainforest where peacock bass crush topwater lures with the force of a strongman wielding a sledge. For others, it is fly-casting for taimen on a subarctic river in a green-and-brown wilderness in Siberia or Mongolia or who knows where. For still others, it is an offshore adventure in Panama to battle blue marlin.

"It," of course, is the destination of the exotic fishing trip every angler dreams about.

For my friends and me in Boardman, Ohio, it was the day every summer when we were granted permission to fish Weller's Pond.

At not much more than two acres, Weller's Pond did not rank with a jungle river or ocean expedition in terms of exoticness. It was accessible via a simple walk through the backyards of neighbors. Total travel time from friend Gary's house was no more than five minutes on foot.

But Weller's Pond might as well have been a thousand miles away. It was off-limits, private property, and we neighbor kids were not inclined to scoff at authority, for fear of confiscation of our precious fishing rods and reels and, worse, a stern punishment at home when parents learned of transgressions. We were not exactly timid, but respectful nonetheless, and even tiptoed across property lines to retrieve batted, thrown, or kicked balls that had strayed into yards where the owners frowned on trespassers. At least, that's what we thought.

The legend of Weller's Pond grew during those long, hot, lazy summers when we got bored with the little fish that swam in Yellow Creek. It was a huge deal when one of us caught a bluegill or crappie. A ten-inch sucker was about as big as the game got during most of our creek trips. Occasionally a bullhead would bite and pull with more strength than we'd become accustomed to fighting.

During dry spells, Yellow Creek might shrivel down to near-zero flow, leaving only a few pools holding water deeper than eight or ten inches. The fishing, obviously, became decidedly tougher as July waned into August and the creek dried up. That pond down the street started looking like it might be worth a sneaky expedition. Perhaps the owners weren't home. Perhaps they wouldn't look out their windows. Perhaps they really wouldn't notice four or five preteens fishing in their backyard.

As tempting as it was, we dared not go where we were forbidden.

One day, however, one of the fishing buddies learned we might be granted permission to fish Weller's Pond. I cannot recall who picked up that intelligence or who mustered up the brass to ask, but word went out: we could fish tomorrow at Weller's Pond.

The morning of our Weller's Pond adventure arrived. With lofty goals in mind, we dug more intently for the plumpest and wiggliest worms. Bait secured, we gathered at Gary's house. Then the four of us paraded to the pond, each with one hand dangling a spinning rod and the other clutching a bait can. This, we surmised, was the day when fishing would be like nothing we'd ever experienced before.

But we were newbies at Weller's Pond—and knew next to nothing about reading the water of something so massive as a two-acre pond. On that day more than fifty years ago, I had yet to gain what I call "fish sense."

Today, I can call on experience. I know with reasonable certainty where a largemouth might be lurking or a bluegill might be hiding. More often than not while bass fishing today, I am looking toward the shoreline. I have an affinity for skinny-water tactics and have refined an approach that centers on high-potential targets in water less than four or five feet deep. My backside points to the open water while my eyes are scanning the bank.

That day we punched our ticket to Weller's Pond, however, I lacked the five decades of seasoning that eventually taught me my best chances for a largemouth bass are within twenty-five feet of where the waves lap the sand, mud, or rocks. The Great Weller's Pond Expedition featured four young boys launching worms on hooks hung under red-and-white bobbers as far out from shore as possible. Out there, we surmised, big bass were waiting for our arrival.

Or so we thought. If the bass were indeed out there, they were not impressed by our baits. As near as I can remember, none of us hooked up with a bass. We probably rationalized, figuring we had the wrong bait or the bass just weren't in a biting mood.

Our day on the pond was not a failure, however, as we did manage to catch a bunch of bluegills, the spunky and colorful panfish that are the gateway species for many of us who call ourselves anglers. They bit willingly and fought more tenaciously than the chubs we busied ourselves with during our normal trips to Yellow Creek.

In hindsight, it was probably a good thing that we did not catch bass during our big day on the pond. Early success might have spoiled me. Instead, I set a new goal. I vowed to return someday. I would read my fishing magazines and learn more about the wily largemouth bass, and when my next opportunity to trek over to Weller's Pond arrived, I would be ready to capitalize.

Little did I know then, of course, that is the mindset of every successful angler. I learned a whole lot more that hot summer day on Weller's Pond than I could have imagined.

CHAPTER 9

Game fish in the eye of the beholder

Is a carp a game fish to a trout angler? Is a bass worthy for a muskie man?

Questions for the ages from the ages. When I was a youngster, my favorite fish to catch was whichever was the biggest in Yellow Creek, a short bicycle ride from the house where I grew up.

It might have been a sucker that cruised the shallow pools in search of bottom life like insect larvae, crawfish, or bits of terrestrial life washed into the creek in the last rainstorm. It might have been a chub, sprouting knobby "horns" on its head. A few of them grew to a size that made them feisty fighters after falling for the garden worms we floated through their hiding holes. Or it might have been a foot-long bullhead, the yellow-bellied bewhiskered fish that skimmed the silted creek bottom in search of anything the chubs and suckers left behind.

But if we had a chance to fish in one of the ponds whose owners occasionally granted permission, our preferred catch shifted to bluegills, crappies, and the biggest game children might imagine—largemouth bass. What a thrill to catch a bass! It would fuel our fishing fire for weeks.

While children can discover glee in catching almost any species of fish, adults often develop preferences. Their preferences can grow into prejudices that cause them to look with disdain on fish that they judge as not worthy of their angling efforts.

A good case in point is the utter disgust expressed by anglers who catch freshwater drum while targeting walleyes on Lake Erie. The drum goes by many names: sheepshead, gaspergou, silver bass, and a few that are less complimentary. They grow large and fight hard thanks to their wide bodies and broom-shaped tails. Reeling in a three-pound drum might take twice as long as a three-pound walleye, but to a walleye angler the drum is a complete waste of time.

Likewise, a Lake Erie angler targeting smallmouth bass will make insulting comments at the realization the fish on the end of the line is a sheepshead. Never mind that the fish might scale up to eight or ten pounds. Catching it is just time ill spent, many would say.

Wife Barb once hooked a fish so large she couldn't curb its initial run. The little reel on her ultralight outfit screeched as the drag tried with all its might to wear down the big fish. The situation was approaching critical when I pulled the anchor and powered the electric trolling motor to chase the fish. It really looked for a while like the fight would end with the reel spooled, and I really didn't want to leave a fish in the lake with a hundred yards of monofilament dangling from its mouth.

Gradually, the battle turned. I spelled Barb several times when her arms tired under the strain of pulling against the fish. More than a half hour after Barb set the hook—and a quarter mile from the point where we'd dropped anchor—the big fish finally surfaced. It was a carp, a huge

A carp like this is a magnificent fighter, but some anglers curse
carp as less than game fish caliber.

specimen at that. It bottomed out a twenty-pound spring scale I kept in the boat. When we finally boated the beast, we weren't surprised by its species. We had set out that evening to catch carp. Intentionally. On purpose.

Game fish are so-called because they fight long and hard, giving anglers their money's worth in each and every encounter.

So who says a carp isn't a game fish?

Don't tell that to carp tournament anglers. Popular in Great Britain and elsewhere around the world, carp competitions attract a lot of attention. Pockets of interest also have developed in the US. But for the most part, people who target carp for sport are judged by other game fish anglers to be a bit odd.

But then again, people who love walleye fishing often consider anglers who love other species a bit odd. Bass anglers too are so glued to their favorite species that they eschew encounters with nonbass. Some snobby trout anglers think it isn't fishing if it isn't floating a dry fly for a wary rainbow or brown; they'll tell you an angler who drifts a nymph is a Neanderthal.

Game fish, for many, are in the eye of the beholder. One angler's prize is another angler's trash.

Fortunately for fishing, plenty of anglers still thrill at any and all fish they catch. Fishing's ranks include those who go to the lake with night crawlers, minnows, topwater lures, in-line spinners and jigs, and everything but the kitchen sink. They are ready for whatever might swim within range of their casts.

CHAPTER 10

Fishing in our complicated world

Perhaps you are among those who read the news or scan social media and sometimes wonder whether our society can be any more divided.

I can tell you I do. Sometimes I wonder why in the world folks feel so hard-pressed to let others know what they think of this or that—especially on things that really don't matter much.

A fishing-themed meme made the rounds recently on social media. Meant to be a joke, the meme insinuated that those who fish for a certain species are more manly than those who pursue another.

Sure, it was a gag. Many laughed, including me.

But the meme reminded me how easily we can find reasons to disagree. Then, later that day, the Super Bowl broadcast really drove home that point.

During the game, a Bud Light TV commercial spoofed MillerCoors for using corn syrup in its light beer. My first reaction was that it was a funny way to differentiate Bud Light from its archrival brews. But America's corn farmers weren't amused. All manner of outrage made headlines and tore through Twitter.

Are you kidding me?

The way I see it, fish are fish and sugar is sugar. If you want to fish for bass or walleyes or whatever, I'm fine with that. If you want to make your beer with malted barley, rice, or corn syrup, I'm OK with that too.

Our world is pretty complicated, however, and many people don't shrug away sarcastic jabs quite so easily. I've come to learn some anglers really do think they are fishing a cut above the crowd because they specialize in bass.

Some anglers think you are a barbarian if your idea of fishing is to put a piece of meat on a hook and hang it under a bobber.

They would tell you fishing is an art form that qualifies its practitioner as an angler only if he or she ties on a dry fly, delivers it to the water on a wisp of gossamer, and floats it flawlessly over the head of a trout with an appetite only for the insects native to its stream.

In a world where people relish showing how they are special, even we anglers are not immune from being just a little too smug about why we do what we do.

I enjoy fishing for bass. Sometimes I wonder whether I enjoy it maybe more than I should. It is entirely possible I miss some mighty fine opportunities to catch fish more willing to cooperate because I'm so focused on those doggone bass.

The funny fishing meme got me to thinking about the prejudices we carry through our days—even (or maybe especially) on the water. The Bud Light Super Bowl commercial only underscored the notion that one person's sweet sugar is another person's pure poison.

Rarely is right or wrong as clear as we think it is. Are you a better person if you fish for a fancy trout or a mighty muskie instead of a bottom-feeding catfish or a humble rock bass?

Recently I noticed another fishing meme on Facebook. It was a picture of a bluegill with a caption that read: "The gateway drug of the fishing world."

Now that makes sense. Who among anglers didn't start fishing with a tiny hook baited with a worm or cricket hanging under a bobber over a bevy of bluegills?

Sometimes I wonder why we make things so complicated.

CHAPTER 11
Coping with the coronavirus

The sun was rising when I sat down to write this. I am always optimistic at that time of the day because the day is full of promise. That's one of the reasons why I love to get an early start on my fishing days.

I go fishing often, sometimes three or even four days a week now that I have retired from my days in an office. Today I have other plans, but I did go fishing yesterday, and I made some very interesting observations.

Talk about a complicated world. When I wrote the previous chapter, we'd never heard about coronavirus, COVID-19, shelter in place, or social distancing. "Global pandemic" was the stuff of tense, terrifying fiction. Michael Crichton's *The Andromeda Strain* comes to mind.

But today as I write this, the world is different and people are coping with the uncertainties around us, scary stuff that most could never have imagined mere months ago. COVID-19 leaped out of a dark closet that never should have been opened and spread suffering, death, and fear around the world in a matter of weeks.

Everything changed for humankind in the first months of 2020. Literally everything was disrupted. But people have a natural tendency to adapt to the circumstances. We just want normal, and we go to great lengths to achieve it.

Fishing is normal. And fishing was among the early activities that became acceptable and popular as relief from the tedium of imposed isolation. Just about the time many of us were totally fed up with staying secluded in our homes, the weather broke and fishing beckoned. Many states concurred that fishing was OK as long as anglers practiced social distancing.

So we went to the rivers, lakes, and oceans and escaped the awful feeling of helplessness that creeps into our souls after weeks and weeks away from workplaces, schools, restaurants, and houses of worship. We were unable to visit stores, zoos, amusement parks, museums, theaters, concert venues, stadiums, arenas, and most every other place people go for fun and entertainment.

But we could go fishing. Hallelujah!

The day before I sat down to write this, I was on the lake and experienced the joy of a fishing trip. It reminded me that I ought to never take a fishing day for granted.

Before the virus, who would have ever thought going to a grocery store would be a high-stakes endeavor with serious infection as a possible outcome? Who would have thought dining out with friends or enjoying craft beer with buddies at a brewery was impossible? Who would have guessed no school in America would hold a traditional commencement for graduating seniors?

But as I fished yesterday, it occurred to me that I was fortunate to have angling as a distraction. On the water, I did not think about social distancing, scrubbing my hands while singing "Happy Birthday," or whether somebody had sneezed in my space.

Yesterday was me, the lake, and the fish. That's the way it always is when I go fishing. It was my version of normal.

I noticed others were equally occupied by their own fishing efforts.

From my perch on the front deck of my boat, I saw a man wading knee deep along the distant shoreline with a spinning rod in his hands. A shirtless man sat nearby, gazing at the floats that suspended his baits off the bottom with hope that a crappie or catfish might find them.

As I maneuvered around the shoreline in search of targets at which to aim my casts, I glanced out across the lake and observed several boats with anglers working a break line for walleyes.

A fleet of muskie anglers worked hard to hook up, their target species apparent based on the speed-trolling tactics they employed.

Joining the action were numerous boats with men and women teamed in a couples bass tournament.

I saw anglers fishing from expensive boats and from homemade rigs. I saw canoes and kayaks and people sitting on the ends of their docks.

Everybody was fishing that day—or so it seemed because fishing was my own distraction on a day when I would rather not worry about the necessities of staying out of harm's way.

Normal will return someday. But in the meantime, I will seize those moments when fishing will put me in a very happy place.

CHAPTER 12
Me, myself, and I

Most of what we do is better with friends. I don't enjoy a solo round of golf. On the rare occasion when I have dined at a table for one on business trips, I felt an awkward need to eat and run. I have never gone to a movie theater without someone I know in the seat next to me. Even sipping a beer on the porch is more enjoyable when I have someone with whom I can share a tale or two.

But I am happy to fish by myself. I actually find it delightful.

Earlier, we celebrated the great friendships strengthened on my boats over the years. But I often fish alone. With me, myself, and I aboard, the skipper is free to roam the waters without the concerns of others to consider.

Eight hours of singular existence on the water is a cathartic experience. I know of no better way to put matters in perspective.

Barb worries that my solo trips on the boat are not good ideas. She has grounds. I've had a few mishaps. But so far, I've returned home intact.

When I go to the lake, I am never without a goal. Pursuing that goal is best done without distractions. I'm not saying I amble aimlessly while fishing with friends, but it is possible that while talking sports, politics, or business, one might get a bit sideways en route to hitting the day's target.

Distractions don't come so easily when I'm out there solo. My senses are tuned, and I'm alert to signals. I simply pay more attention fishing alone.

Paying close attention means I notice whether that last bass was at the base of a sunken tree or suspended in its limbs. I detect the shift of the wind. I sense the sun is approaching the top of its daily arc over the lake. I hear a fish splash, a deer snort, and a turkey gobble. I smell the rain that I cannot yet see.

I listen to the signals better when it is only me and the water. So all I see, feel, hear, and smell comes together to inform my strategy, tactics, and, ultimately, success.

Does a snorting deer or gobbling turkey say anything to the hearing angler? I say yes. When the animals of the land and the air are active, they are responding to conditions that are not so readily detected by people.

Barometric pressure, the relative positions of the sun and the moon, wind direction, cloud cover, and many other factors play roles in the moment-to-moment behavior of all manner of animal life. That includes

The author loves going to the water solo, but sometimes a friend would be helpful.

mammals, reptiles, birds, people, and, of course, fish.

So when the turkeys are talking in the woods across the bay, the otters are playing on the bank, and the ospreys are spiraling over the water on the morning thermals, I factor that into my day's tactics. When a deer is sipping along the shoreline at high noon, I believe that is a signal worth noting.

Factors that influence air-breathing animals' behavior penetrate the water's surface. Solar and lunar pull, the barometer, the wind and clouds, and more all play roles in fish activity. While most species are decidedly opportunistic about eating (that is, they eat when food shows itself), they do have periods when hunting herring and stalking crawfish are not high priorities.

I am not a scientist, so consider that my interpretation of my observations may be skewed toward what I want them to be rather than being based on the facts of nature. But I have noticed that when I detect more-than-normal animal activity on the shore and in the air, the fish also are on the prowl. And when that happens, I put the clues and cues in my cranial computer so that it can spit out a game plan for winning.

It pays to pay attention, and it is easier to do that when we are focused only on the world around us. It's just easier to keep my focus when the only talking is me muttering to myself.

Fishing alone also is relaxing.

While it is possible for two people to fish side by side without distracting each other, that is no easy feat. People are social. Talking is a strong instinct. So we chat, share stories, tell jokes, ask for ideas, worry about each other's comfort, and all manner of other stuff. Frankly, it can be exhausting.

I need all the energy I can muster for eight hours on the water. It's easier to conserve energy when the only person with whom I must concern myself is me.

Fact is I return from a solo trip feeling recharged. It's like my body's battery absorbed more energy than it expended.

With mind clear and body rejuvenated after a day on the lake, I can be more productive with business back at home—like planning for my next fishing trip.

CHAPTER 13

In a word . . . say what?

Every sport has its jargon. Fishing is no exception. We anglers speak a language well understood by our buddies but that might as well be gibberish to those who do not possess the proper glossary.

I laugh out loud sometimes at the terms we utter in describing situations, techniques, and strategies. It all sounds so serious and scientific. It makes us sound as though we are pretty well on top of our game, if not occupying even higher rungs on the ladder of life.

Truth is, that's what jargon accomplishes. If you are a chef and you are describing the finer points of the sous vide cooking technique, it sounds pretty special—a whole lot more special than to say you will boil your meat in a plastic bag.

Google "jargon" and you will see a definition that declares jargon is "special words or expressions that are used by a particular profession or group and are difficult for others to understand." Indeed.

Many years ago I wrote a feature about jargon for a magazine and learned from a professor whose doctorate thesis was on the topic of jargon and vulgarities. That jargon and swear words were his focus makes sense from the fishing perspective. Four-letter words pepper the sad stories of the big ones that got away.

A person who strolls the dock at a lake where a fishing tournament has just concluded might very well hear a competitor explaining his or her day on the water: "The prespawners were staging off the break line where I boxed a limit on lipless cranks."

Staging? A longtime tournament teammate cracked up every time he heard an angler declare the bass were staging. "What exactly does that mean, and how do we know they are staging?" he would invariably ask. He would then share the image that popped into his head: a trio of bass in top hats and little tuxedos, dancing to stage left on their tail fins while twirling canes with their dorsal fins. That, he declared, is staging.

Nevertheless, bass anglers who talk about staging fish are well understood by their peers.

I could offer a glossary of fishing jargon, but it would be woefully inadequate to cover the gamut of terms that have become part of the vernacular of those who love their fishing. Nevertheless, I offer a few bits of popular jargon and their translations.

Lunker: The term has been used for more than a hundred years to describe a large fish, but nobody these days is exactly sure of its roots. Some also describe big fish with words that end in "zilla," in homage to science fiction's Godzilla. A huge trout, for example, might be called "troutzilla." Another synonym is "biggin." The term rolls off the tongues of excited anglers like a song lyric, but the word hits other ears like fingernails on a chalkboard. My wife, Barb, literally plugs her ears when TV fishermen get jazzed about a big fish and jabber that they've got a biggin on the line. Other big-fish terms include "toad"—but really, is a toad huge?— and "hawg" (isn't the conventional spelling descriptive enough?).

Toothy critter: Elsewhere in this book, I write about those who pursue apex predators like muskies, northern pike, and other fish that have big teeth and voracious appetites. They are the fish that have a fighting chance of inflicting pain on the anglers who catch them, due to their sharp teeth. Collectively, muskies, pike, and other dagger-tooth species are known as "toothy critters."

Stick: It's a fishing pole, as well as an accomplished angler. The term harks back to the days when an angler might affix a string to a stick and use it to dangle bait in front of nearby fish. Today's "sticks" are a whole lot more sophisticated and often cost one hundred dollars or more. We also describe successful fishers as "good sticks," which means they probably have a lot of those expensive sticks at their disposal.

Crankbait: I love this term. It is used to identify a wide range of hard-body lures. Before I had a lot of experience as a bass fisherman, I would have called them "plugs" because that is the word my father and grandfather would have used. But sometime in the late 1960s, anglers started calling plugs "crankbaits." It is an apt term for sure because to fish them, anglers cast them out and crank them back. A sister term is "spinnerbait." You might guess that this genre of lures includes components that spin—and you would be correct.

Salad: Some salads are made with lettuce or potatoes and mayonnaise. Others are made from beets and carrots. Still others feature gelatin as the main feature. But for the most part, salads are built around leafy green plants. So when anglers say they are catching them in the "salad," they are referring to aquatic vegetation, aka "weed beds" or "grass beds."

Walking the dog: Did you have a yo-yo when you were a kid? A popular yo-yo trick called "walking the dog" featured the yo-yo spinning from the string perpendicular to the operator's hand but not climbing back up the string. "Walking the dog" in fishing is completely different. It is a style of retrieve that an angler uses with a topwater lure that causes the lure to dart left and right repeatedly while covering relatively little linear distance. The result is the lure remains active and enticing while hovering over the strike zone for a prolonged period of time.

So imagine, "Joe is a strong stick who targets lunkers while they are staging in the salad, where crankbaits will get snagged but walking the dog with a topwater will tease the toothy critters into striking."

Thousands of other terms are in the fishing vernacular. I've explained only a few. But you get the picture, right? Now you are in the "in" crowd when it comes to talking the talk.

CHAPTER 14

If docks could talk

All lakes have them. The floating wooden platforms are ubiquitous on lakes from the tundra to the equator in nearly every nation on earth. They allow people to tread out over deeper water, to secure their boats, and to enjoy the serenity that is the unspoken promise of lakescapes worldwide.

Serenity, huh? If docks could talk, they would tell us of all manner of human error, conflict, and chaos. You know Murphy's Law: if something can go wrong, it will.

But the docks on any given lake also are hubs of fishing activities. Anglers use them to reach well out into the water, where they suspect favored fish reside. They tie their boats to docks to load and unload, and lug dripping stringers of fresh-caught fish across the docks to landside coolers or fillet tables.

The docks on lakes are there to soak in all that and then some.

Picture the dock. It is a workhorse that serves the people who go to the water. It readily shows its age, its weathered wood gray and worn. Docks may even be vengeful. They are capable of delivering a painful splinter to the careless barefoot shuffler. Slippery when wet, docks can send a clumsy angler or boater sliding into the water. Put too much weight on one side of the dock and you just might end up swimming.

Lucky is the lakeside dock positioned where people flock. They are the ones that see and hear all. Visit any boat ramp and you'll soon see what I am saying.

Just because a person has the wherewithal to buy a boat doesn't necessarily mean he has the skills required to get it into the water. Marina docks bear witness every day of the summer to hours of the kind of "Boat Ramp Follies" enjoyed by millions of YouTube viewers.

I've been there myself countless times when people launched their boat with drain plugs missing. Oops.

I was there back in the day when people drove station wagons to tow their boats. A boater carefully backed his trailer into the water, hopped out to pull the boat to the dock, and watched helplessly as his Buick continued in reverse. The car slowly submerged to the point where only the hood ornament was dry. Oops.

The docks say nothing, but they see and hear.

They don't laugh (out loud, anyway) at the hapless drivers who, regardless of how many times they try, simply are unable to back a trailer down a ramp without jackknifing the rig. They stifle a chuckle when a poor soul races to keep up with a tow-vehicle driver who pulls up out of the water after instructing his helper to hold the rope.

Docks don't cry when the anglers who stand on them lose a good fish at the net. Nor do they shed a tear when a stringer of crappies somehow comes undone from the cleat to which it was secured.

They see everything, but say nothing. That cannot be easy. Maybe that's a factor in how quickly their wood turns from fresh to shades of gray.

I am pretty certain the dock cringed the day a very angry man screamed at my friend and me from his weathered wooden platform and threw gravel at our boat as we fished nearby. I would guess the docks cover their ears to block the bickering of families stressed by the rigors of launching and loading their boats. And I hope they don't hold a grudge against the numbskulls who create boat-ramp gridlock when they occupy the slip that many others could be using until the time when their own trailer finally arrives.

But it's not all gloom and doom for the docks on our lakes.

When the sky is sunny, the air warm, and the wind favorable, a boat dock is a perfect venue for children to learn the joys of fishing. Children giggle with glee for even the slightest of reasons while fishing out on the end of an old gray dock. Siblings assist as the youngest learn the ropes, while parents shepherd their flock to make sure none get too close

A weathered boat dock has many tales to share.

to the edge. Grandparents beam as they soak up the wonder their new generation is experiencing.

The days when families are out are special, even for the old dock that has been there, done that.

Earlier I mentioned "If docks could talk." Who knows for sure? Perhaps they can. So I can imagine an old floating wooden dock, its color and grain showing the character of age and experience. Way out on the end is an equally weathered Adirondack chair, its yellow paint faded enough to reveal rusty nailheads still, but barely, keeping the arms attached in place. The day is hot. The air is still. At the water's edge, where the pavement slides off into the lake, a man is backing his boat trailer for launch.

"Hey, Chair, did you see that?" asked Dock.

"Yep. That's the third time that guy has scraped the trailer fender on your float," replied Chair. "Did the same last week. Took him three tries to get it straight."

"Yeah, Chair, and did you hear what he said? Such language!"

"Yep. Good thing the kids who fish out here weren't around today."

Indeed. If docks could talk, they would have plenty to say.

CHAPTER 15

The most worrisome snag of all time

If you have fished, you have experienced the frustration of a snagged hook. It's an outcome as much a part of fishing as baiting, casting, and catching. As a matter of fact, I have had days when my lure was snagged on the bottom of the lake or in a bush or tree limb more often than being stuck in a fish's mouth.

Snags are vexing, for sure. They are, however, easily overcome. Usually. But not always.

The stuff we tie to the ends of our lines can be dangerous weapons, considering they feature needle-sharp hooks and are heavy enough that when jerked free of a snag they can slingshot back toward the anglers wielding them.

Almost everyone I know has been snagged by his or her own lure. That is part of the price of admission in fishing. Ninety percent of the hook sticks suffered by anglers are easily tended at the scene. A few, however, need to visit an emergency medical center to have the offending hooks cut out.

A fisher friend of mine lost sight in one eye after the spinner he was fishing snagged. As all of us do in such circumstances, he jerked on the stuck bait. It pulled free and hurtled like a bullet back toward his face, where it punched into his eye and caused permanent damage. He normally would have been wearing polycarbonate sunglasses, which would have protected his eyes, but he had removed them so that he could see better under the bridge where he was fishing.

Freak accidents are always a threat when we go to the water. A misstep here, a bump there, a flopping fish, an electric spark and—boom—you find yourself in a jackpot.

I suffered my share of minor injuries and scary close calls while fishing my way through season after season. I break out an alcohol swab and bandage or rub a little ice on the boo-boo and get back to fishing a bit wiser and more attentive.

One of those freak accidents really put me in a worry.

It was a breezy, bright October day, and the bass were in a feeding mood. They were chasing down shallow-running crankbaits worked along rock and sand points and wiggled down the trunks of trees that leaned from the bank out into the lake. Bass after bass blasted the lure as it caromed and careened like a bewildered shad fleeing a predator.

Anglers' lures snag often. This one created a real
predicament for the author.

Occasionally, of course, the treble hooks stuck in the waterlogged wood or wedged in a rocky crevice. Each time, I succeeded in freeing the lure and returned to fishing and catching.

It was the kind of day when an angler sighs and smiles, satisfied he or she made the right decision about going to the lake.

Then my lure got snagged again. I tried the usual tricks, like plucking the line as if it were the string on a bow, reversing the direction of my tugs, and finally reeling straight down to put my rod tip in direct contact with the split ring on the crankbait.

Nothing worked. This particular snag was the kind we all dread. The only way to get back to fishing was to break the line, it seemed. Then I noticed I could see the lure. Its chartreuse flank was just bright enough to pierce the murk. I realized I could maneuver the boat overtop the snagged bait, grab it barehanded, and pull it free.

I reached for the bait, got a grip, and tugged. Nothing. So I tugged more. Still nothing. I resigned to give one final, mighty tug before surrendering and leaving the bait stuck to the snag. I tugged hard and my fingers slipped . . . but I couldn't bring my hand to the surface.

My hand was elbow deep and stuck fast to one of the treble hooks. Facts started to become evident. The snag was a snarl of nylon rope. The wind was blowing in a direction that was pulling the boat away from the snag. I had no pliers or knife within reach of the hand that was not stuck to the bottom of the lake. And I soon realized the hook penetration was a through-and-through wound, with the barb in a location that meant the only way out was to rip against the web skin between my index and middle fingers.

Options? Stay there until help arrived, but with my skin serving as the secure point for a boat tethered in place, that seemed to be a daunting prospect. Plus, I'd seen only a couple of other boats on the lake that day. I could crawl over the gunnel into the lake and use my free hand and feet to pull the snarled rope free of where it was snagged to the bottom. But the boat no doubt would drift far out into the lake by the time I freed myself, and swimming to retrieve it was not an option. Or I could rip my hand away from the hook and suffer whatever damage that might cause to my skin.

I went with ripping first. That's when I learned human skin is as tough as cowhide. Try as I might, I couldn't rip the quarter inch of skin between the hook's entry and exit points.

So you may be thinking about pain at this point, right?

No pain, at least in the physical sense. The pain was in my head as I struggled with how freaky this situation was and whether I might actually survive it. I was in a part of the lake where the shoreline is wild. Nobody ever goes there on foot. If no other boater happened to pass near, how long would I be moored in a very vulnerable position?

It was chilly, but I was sweating.

Five minutes passed, then ten and twenty. I was flat on my belly, spread-eagle on the deck, with my right hand over the side. Stress was beginning to overpower the initial shock when I spied a pair of needle-nose pliers on the deck. They were out of reach of my free hand, but if I could maneuver my foot just so, I could drag the pliers close enough to grab.

Tool in hand, I reached for the treble hook embedded in the cursed nylon rope. I pulled, and the pliers slipped. I pulled again, and bingo, my hand was free. I pulled my hand out of the water, sat up, and saw the lure dangling between my knuckles. Now able to get the pliers properly positioned to get enough leverage, I mashed the barb, and the hook slid easily out of the two holes in my skin.

I keep a first aid kit aboard for cuts and scrapes. I opened an alcohol swab, cleaned up the wound, and applied a bandage.

I thought about going home to lick my wounds and count my blessings. Instead I resumed fishing. But not before I replaced the hook damaged by my mashing of its barb.

Wouldn't you do the same?

CHAPTER 16

You gotta hold your mouth just right

Two friends are fishing. One's catching them regularly. The other is just soaking bait. What's up with that?

Since the first people to fish stood next to each other on the banks of antiquity, some succeeded more often than the others. Some failed regularly, while others seemingly could not keep the fish off their hooks.

I have stood waist-deep in rushing water casting jigs for spring-run walleyes and white bass and watched in awe as the person twenty feet from me hooked up twice as often as I hooked up.

I've been on boats out in the trackless expanse of big water, drifting across a featureless flat with six pals and the skipper. The walleye were down there, as we could plainly see by the blips on the sonar display, but some of us caught them and some did not.

Many are the days when I shared a boat with a buddy. We fished long days, barely fifteen feet from each other, but one of us usually scored more than the other.

Many reasons can be offered to explain why one person catches them and another does not. One fellow once told me, "You gotta hold your mouth just right." Right.

Don't discount luck. It is a factor. But truth be told, anglers who consistently catch fish tend to bring more to the game than long odds. So while it is true that a bait might sink by happenstance in front of a waiting fish, a good percentage of anglers possess the instinct and experience that provide the platform on which they build their success. They "make" their own luck.

Don't discount stinkiness. The angler who gassed up the boat on the way to the lake and sloshed a little fuel on his or her hands will transfer the odor. Reel handles, fishing line, and lures can hold traces of gasoline that fish can readily smell. The human scent itself also alerts animals that a threat may be imminent, which is why hunters (and an increasing number of anglers) go to great lengths to wash and mask their scents.

Don't discount position. Fishing, as in real estate, has three principles: location, location, and location. The distance to our casting targets, the angle of our presentation, even the knowledge of where the targets are located all play into the fateful moment when a lure lands in an area that

Veteran angler Ray Halter knows a trick or two to catch
more fish than many of his peers.

prompts a waiting game fish to react. Eat or defend? Or ignore and turn away?

Don't discount the secret knowledge an angler might possess. Sure, we love to see our friends enjoy their time with us on the water. But the plain truth is that if I know of a certain stump in a certain part of the lake, a stump that cannot be seen because it's just under the water but at a location I've memorized, am I going to make my cast to that stump without telling my friend to cast there first? You can bet I will.

Don't discount sheer determination. I cannot count how many times I have had determination work in my favor. The angler who believes he or she will catch a fish will catch more than the angler who goes to the water with doubts. If you have a high degree of confidence that a fish lives in the shadow of a log or on the edge of a ledge, you will make more casts and more precise presentations to the cover or structure than fishers who have convinced themselves there are no fish in the lake.

Don't discount attention to detail. The line we select, the knots we tie, the lures we choose, the rods and reels we use, and the locations we select all add up during a day on the water. Attention to detail is one of the most important factors in fishing. It's one of the few factors anglers can control. A sloppy knot, a poor lure choice, a balky reel, and a haphazard presentation can cost us the opportunity to convert bites into catches.

Don't discount the skill with which the angler maneuvers the lure. Fish often see or otherwise sense a lure or bait in their neighborhood before they react. Videos of fish strikes show many game fish observing baits for some time prior to opening their mouths to eat. Often it was a twitch imparted by the angler at a critical moment that caused the fish to strike. A skillful twitch, quiver, jerk, hop, or pause can be the difference between hookup and hauling water. They inform whether your bait looks real or bogus.

And finally, don't discount an unknown force that somehow, down in the depths, directs a bass, walleye, tuna, or tarpon to your lure at the expense of your friend's.

As the saying goes, that is why they call it fishing and not catching.

CHAPTER 17

She's my boat

Fishing boats today are modern marvels with enough bells and whistles to make our grandparents' heads spin.

My maternal grandfather, John Kish, was a tinkerer. He spent countless hours in his workshop fiddling and fussing with gadgets and projects. Never satisfied, he sought ways to make things work better.

Grandpa Kish also built boats, counting on my father for assistance with the Chris-Craft kits he assembled in his garage at home in the 1950s. To stay busy in his later years, he noodled up a boat bumper manufacturing business, handcrafting tens of thousands of the fenders and peddling them to marinas and boat dealers from Detroit to Buffalo.

He loved a well-made functional tool. He was long gone before modern fishing boats hit the water, but had Grandpa had the opportunity to check them out, he would have been mightily impressed.

Today's rigs are equipped like high-performance cars compared with the boats of days gone by. Grandpa couldn't have imagined—or maybe he could—the features and accessories available these days.

He would have been like a kid in a candy store checking out Powerpoles, electric trolling motors, sonar, GPS, outboard engines, stainless props, overstuffed buckets, pedestal seats, elevated carpeted casting decks, hydraulic steering, aerated recirculating livewells, sleek designs, and custom-quality colors and finishes.

Today's fishing boats are species-specific. We have walleye boats, crappie boats, muskie boats, bay boats, offshore boats, and, of course, bass boats—all adorned with amazing accessories.

The cool thing about that stuff is it isn't gingerbread. It all helps us anglers catch fish.

Many of us recall the days when a "fishing" boat was a fourteen-foot aluminum skiff with two or three bench seats and a little outboard pushing out ten or fewer horses. We kept bait in a bucket that sloshed on the floor. Our rods and net clattered around with the oars and anchor.

As I walk around my bass boat, I can make a mental inventory of the features Grandpa would have admired.

Chief among them would be the Powerpoles and MotorGuide trolling motor. The shallow-water anchor Powerpoles combine hydraulics and articulating appendages to deploy and grip the lake bottom for stopping power as I ease along with the electric trolling motor. Grandpa would have appreciated the precise boat-positioning benefits they deliver.

He also would have marveled at the electronics. Sonar tells me exactly what is under the boat, while GPS tells me exactly how to find my way on the water—both so important I can hardly imagine fishing without them.

Grandpa could never have imagined a boat and motor capable of running 60 miles per hour to his favorite spots, but he would have thrilled to feel the wind in his face while sitting secure in a bottom-hugging, spine-cushioning bucket seat.

He most certainly would have appreciated the plumbing job that ensures fresh, aerated water runs through the onboard livewell system to keep his fish lively instead of dragging them around all day on a stringer tied to a cleat.

As I finished my walk-around, I gained new appreciation. We are fortunate to live in a time when fishing boats make our precious hours on the water more enjoyable.

It's also cool that new stuff comes along every year to make our boats better. Grandpa might even have tinkered up a gadget or two to add fish to my livewell.

For an angler as avid as I have been for all of my adult life, I have owned only a few boats. Many friends have owned a dozen or more during the time I've owned three. In my case, I think my unwillingness to swap up for newer and bigger boats has been a bonus in my fishing life. Never mind that I also cannot afford to change boats as often as I change socks, I believe I've benefited by making a special connection with the three vessels that have taken me fishing.

The first boat that I could call mine was a fifteen-foot Arrowglass tri-hull runabout. I'd gone to the mall with wife Barb to buy shoes and stepped right into a late-winter boat show in the concourse. We returned home with visions of that boat etched in our heads. Later that week, we signed the papers for our little red beauty, without even thinking where we might park it. We did not own a home, and our apartment building parking lot was a bit too public for us to feel good about parking the boat there. Barb's parents never said so, but I think they thought we had made a foolish decision.

Nevertheless, we've had a boat in our driveway for all of the years of our marriage. We're fortunate we see things like this in the same light. In our early years of boat ownership, Barb was along on most of the trips. Her fishing trips dropped to two or three in the summer once our daughter arrived, but she dearly enjoyed fishing with little Betsy.

Today, Barb likes to go out on the boat, but not before the sun rises and never in the rain. She was aboard once when sleet pelted our faces, but only once. Often as not these days, Barb is just as happy to set up a golf game with her friends when I'm going fishing. She is interested in my trips, I know, because she always asks where I'm going in case she must alert the sheriff if I don't get home at a reasonable hour.

That old Arrowglass was underpowered, with a 35-horsepower Johnson hanging on the stern. It had no trim and tilt, so wherever I set the bar is where the outboard pushed. After a few years, we upgraded to a 60-horsepower Evinrude, but it still was a pretty basic—and plodding—vessel.

Regardless, it did a very good job getting Barb and me out to the places where we might fish for walleyes and crappies. We took it on Lake Erie a few times and motored up and down the Ohio River. After eighteen years, I sold it to a man who was very excited to take it home and introduce his own young son to fishing. That made me happy.

Its place in my driveway was taken by a seventeen-foot Ranger fish and play boat. By the time I acquired the Ranger, my fishing was almost entirely for bass. Ranger boats, then and now, are pretty much synonymous with bass fishing. Plus they were the crème de la crème, rather like the Cadillac of fishing boats. I towed it with a Chevy, but she was my Caddie bass boat.

I fished hundreds of bass tournaments in the little red Ranger, its 115-horsepower Mercury only half as fast as the big 225- and 250-horsepower outboards pushing twenty- and twenty-one-foot bass boats past me during the morning blastoffs. She was never the fastest boat in the tournament, but her livewells more often than not were full of largemouth and smallmouth bass. Together we won a few bucks over the years, enough that I could offset my expenses and prevent fishing from eroding my bank account.

Fishing can be a costly passion. One lure today can cost as much as my grandfathers earned in a week. A spool of line may have cost a quarter when they were young; today I buy line for twenty-five bucks a spool. As I write this, magazines are advertising bass boats with price tags exceeding $90,000. Really.

So I've never been one to regularly upgrade boats. The Ranger served for fifteen long and hard seasons. I maneuvered into places that owners of bigger (and more expensive) boats timidly avoided. I wiggled over

Like all of the boats owned by the author, his Bass Cat wears red.

stumps and scraped bottom often. She sported a few scratches when I traded her in, but no doubt is still out there somewhere taking her bass angler owner to a secret honey hole.

Today I drive a Bass Cat. As her sisters before her, the Bass Cat wears red.

I like to think of red as a festive color. I'm very happy when I'm aboard my boat. It's like a party for me, and what better way to celebrate than in red! The Arrowglass and Ranger were red, so when it came time for Barb and me to decide what color the Bass Cat factory should make our boat, red topped our list. The online design tool offered up hundreds of color options and combinations, and the process of deciding took weeks. But at least we knew red was our foundation.

Also like her antecedents, the Bass Cat has been a fish-catching machine. In service a decade now, she has taken me to dozens of lakes and rivers and been a reliable and safe platform for hundreds of fishing adventures.

I say "adventures" with conviction.

Fishing is almost always an adventure, at least in my book. That's why I'm so passionate about fishing. It's always a challenge. It's never easy, but it's always fun. As with any adventure, getting there is as much fun as experiencing the destination, and "getting there" in fishing is more than riding the waves to each hot spot.

As a matter of fact, I'm not sure I will ever actually get there. Deep inside me, I fear that if I ever were to get there, I may get bored.

You may have noticed I have referred to my boats as she. Boats throughout history have been given feminine personae. Some say that's because in the Romance languages, which typically assign nouns as either masculine or feminine, the words for boats are feminine nouns.

I am not sure if this is important in my life as an angler, but I suspect it does contribute to the overall order of things. Nature, we know, does tend to seek to flow to balance.

CHAPTER 18

Eat, breathe, fish

John Breedlove is a man of many interests. He has raced cars, coached soccer, and raised children. He can hit a golf ball a country mile and set up a massive industrial slitter to cut down coils of steel into skinny strips. He also can catch fish with uncanny consistency.

This is a story about John Breedlove, Steelhead Aficionado. As Ohio fisheries managers worked to improve the steelhead fishery in Lake Erie, many anglers learned to cash in on the bonanza. John is among them.

That John works in the steel business is fitting in a fashion, for it is steelhead that help define him as an angler. He can catch walleye, bass, and other fish with the best of them, but he has somehow gained a simpatico relationship with the overstuffed rainbow trout that wander from the rivers of their youth to gorge on the summer bounty of wide-open waters and return annually to the tributary where they were hatched or planted.

To earn his pay, John works for a company that breaks down thirty-ton coils of steel into strips—known as mults—that are used by people who stamp or roll a variety of metal shapes for parts that go into everything from the stapler on your desk to components on your car or truck. That's big work, with heavy machinery powered by enormous energy to deliver forces capable of cutting steel with surgical precision.

When John is not working at his day job, he's checking the internet for fish information, towing his rig to the lake, or fishing. Such dedication often rewards its practitioner with success. It certainly has done so for John Breedlove.

Dedication. Think about that term in your own context. What have you seen accomplished by sheer dedication? Perhaps it is something in your own experience. Or perhaps it is the way your child or your friend's child has become an accomplished guitarist or basketball player or spelling champion.

John is like the spelling bee champion of Ohio steelhead fishermen, and he wears the sash year after year because of his dedication to details that seem almost insignificant to those who are not so dialed in.

It makes sense that a man who can set up a machine to produce precision strips of steel sliced from sixty thousand pounds of coiled metal can tame a powerful wild steelhead trout with seemingly little effort.

To be sure, other anglers can do what John Breedlove does—but not as many as one might guess. John was born in the Steel Valley of Northeast Ohio, not the Pacific Northwest, where young people learn to fish their hometown rivers in Alaska, Washington, Oregon, California, or British Columbia. He grew up near steel mills, an auto assembly plant, and a myriad of other industrial factories, far from snowcapped mountains that channel their melt to rivers that run to the sea. He learned to fish swamp-fed waters for catfish, bluegills, and crappies, not silver or king salmon or ocean-run rainbow trout.

Yet he has an uncanny understanding about how to make steelhead, lake trout, and brown trout strike his lures as they wander from Lake Erie to the rivers and creeks. What's more, he will tell any and all the exact formula for his success. It's as though he delights more in sharing his experiences than in hoarding them. That's not a common trait in the world of fishing, where secret lures and fishy hot spots are as precious as money in the bank or heirlooms in the will.

It's not as though his formula is so general as to be easily guessed. He experiments to get the speed of his lures exactly right for the day's conditions. If the boat should be moving 2.1 mph, he won't settle at 2.0, and he'll feather the throttle as the current ebbs and flows. He will know exactly how far behind the boat his spoons are fluttering. If the fish are hitting eighty-five feet back, that's exactly where his lures are set. Color is critical in John's repertoire, and the amount of orange or blue or purple or chartreuse paint on the spoon is as calculated as his decision to work with gold or chrome plating.

He delights in visual contact with the fish he chases. He deploys a tiny camera between the terminal end of his main line and the leader to which the lure is attached, and records every fish that swims near his lure. He sees follows, turn-aways, and strikes, and can watch on video replay how the fish react and what makes them hot.

While some of us fish in oblivion, John takes control of almost every variable that contributes to each day's success or failure.

The fish hardly have a chance against him. And he wants you to have the same odds. Just ask John and he'll tell you everything.

John Breedlove never tires of the pursuit of more and bigger fish.

CHAPTER 19

Mine's bigger than yours

I am by nature competitive. I loved playing baseball. I played shortstop and loved swinging the bat. A solid hit reverberated into my soul. Each caught pop-up or fielded grounder was another notch of success in the belt I buckled in my brain.

Later I took up racquetball and played countless hours in echoing white rooms with hardwood floors slick with our sweat. An ace serve or a hard low passing shot was fuel enough to drive me to the courts day after day. Golf too has been a favorite game of mine, with the satisfaction of a well-struck shot or a perfectly calculated putt serving as a great reward for the years invested in trying and trying . . . and trying again.

But despite the thrills of a sharp line drive to the gap, a holed wedge shot, or a perfect corner pinch rollout, I really need to know the score when the day is done. How did I do? Did I win? Did someone beat me?

This is why I like competitive fishing.

I started fishing bass tournaments in 1983. I had no idea what I was doing when I recruited a friend to enter a buddy-style bass tournament with me. I'd read a few articles in Bassmaster magazine, but I was a fish out of water when it came to knowing the ins and outs of tournament competition.

I thought I was a pretty good fisherman, and my friend actually caught as many (or more), so I figured we'd be a formidable team.

Turns out I had a lot to learn.

Competitive fishing is a whole different sport. It has hints of the idyllic pastime immortalized by Izaak Walton in his *The Compleat Angler*. Since its first publication, in 1653, *The Compleat Angler* has been a starting point for those who seek to elevate their spirits and celebrate angling as an art form. Which, of course, it is.

Fishing is grace, balance, beauty, shape, and color presented in realism, surrealism, impressionism, and even cubism. It is form and substance in the movement of the angler's choice.

Art is in the eye of the beholder, so we love fishing as much or more for its artistic significance in our souls than for any other reason.

But the truth is anglers do compete. We want sport. We return to our docks happy to show off the results of our day—or hide them from curiosity seekers who would race out on the lake to duplicate our efforts and "steal" the fish we want to catch tomorrow. Two people on the same boat might be inclined to place wagers on the first, biggest, and most fish of the day.

Even out on the mountain streams, where rainbow and brown trout are the dream of anglers wielding long fly rods to present tiny dry flies, the race to the best holes and runs is on before the sun has cleared the eastern horizon.

It makes sense then that a group of anglers with similar equipment, fast boats, and a few dollars to wager might rally around an organizer to determine who is the best bass angler on any given day. That is the basic premise of tournament-style bass fishing.

The day starts early. Well before the first shifts of the local manufacturing plants have clocked in, the launch ramps of lakes and rivers across America are flush with people and boats getting ready for their eight-hour crack at the resident bass population. A thin blue cloud of smoke from outboard engines hangs a couple of feet over the harbor as the contestants pick up boatmates and idle out to await the starter's signal.

Tournament fishing is one part Izaak Walton, one part Daytona 500, one part Baryshnikov ballet, and one part Ali versus Foreman heavyweight slugfest. As the sun rises, we revel in the peace and beauty of nature. Then the race starts and a hundred boats speed away to seek their riches of bass. The dance advances as the competitors cast and retrieve with graceful coordination learned and refined by years of practice. The

Whether we recognize it or not, all anglers have a competitive streak.
Whose fish is bigger? Whose boat is faster? Photo by William D. Lewis

angling combatants go face-to-face with bigmouth quarry that will fight
with fury to resist the anglers' hands.

Tournament fishing has a cast of characters as rich as any competitive
pursuit. Men and women. Young and old. Braggers, perfectionists,
dreamers, and schemers are rank-and-file members of the tournament
movement. They are joined by shy folks, clumsy klutzes, the clueless,
and the curious.

The common denominator is tournament people are motivated to
compare their catch with others. They want to know how their score
compares with those of their peers.

It's a natural thing. By nature, anglers want to show off their fish
and claim title to fishing prowess. Whether the goal is more fish for
the tribe, more trophies for the mantle, or more money in our pockets,
competitive fishing has deep roots in humanity.

So tournament fishing . . . we should have seen it coming.

As a competitor myself, I see competitive fishing as a microcosm
of society. Everyone wants to know the score. Person versus person.
Community versus community. State versus state. Nation versus nation.
Even, it must be said, faith versus faith.

Tournament angling is a community in every bit the same sense as a scout troop, high school, church, and state. The competitive fishing community at-large has subsets, tribes that choose to specialize in bass, walleyes, muskies, billfish, sharks, redfish, or many other species.

Members are linked by their desire to accomplish—in their case capturing and showing their catch in hopes of reaping a reward. The member roster is like that of every other social group.

We have winners and achievers who scout ahead, practice long hours, study maps, and invest heavily in the best and most state-of-the-art goodies and gadgets. They are the first to the lake in the morning and the last to leave at sunset.

We have the Average Joes. They love the game but aren't particularly good at winning. They may notch a first or second on rare occasions, but for the most part they go home with nothing much to show other than a sunburn.

We have the back markers. They show up with enthusiasm every tournament morning, sometimes even with the best boat, motor, rods, and reels that money can buy. But they lack the drive necessary to make success happen. They enjoy saying they are competitive anglers but have no hardware to prove their mettle.

Alas, we also have cheaters. Temptation to cut corners exists in all human societies. Did early people poach apples from their neighboring tribe's trees? Do students look for answers before they even see their tests? Do desperadoes rob banks rather than work honest jobs? Do some anglers on occasion break rules to avoid the embarrassment of defeat or to win money they do not deserve? The answers to each of those questions, of course, is yes.

And so it goes. The challenge is out there. We all want to catch more and bigger fish than our peers.

Mine, my friend, is bigger than yours.

CHAPTER 20

A little more salt, please

The first time I saw a fan ask a fisherman for an autograph, it struck me that fishing can indeed be called a professional sport. Pro anglers can fish for oversized trophies and piles of prize money. They can produce TV shows and boast about the size of their catches to adoring viewers. They can sign promotion contracts with companies that wish to sell their wares to fishers. And they can print business cards, produce websites, and market their fish-finding skills to clients who will pay them to take them fishing.

All of this because they can catch fish. Life's good.

For some who are professional anglers, life is even better when the scent of the sea fills their nostrils. They are the ones who greet the sun with heads already spinning about the bait, the tides, the forecast, and more. Something about saltwater anglers helps set them in their own place—even in the wide world of angling.

I know a number of professional anglers. Some are dudes with million-dollar smiles and a talent for catching bass while working in sleek boats, logo-emblazoned jerseys, and crisply creased pants. Some are Lake Erie skippers whose charter boat clients range from families to party animals to Amish farmers looking to put fish on the table to feed their clans.

And some are people whose workplace is on their small share of the three-quarters of our planet covered by seawater. They are those whose occupation is a little saltier than most. Consider Will Geraghty.

The salt is different, in my mind. The salt is where fishing is grittier.

It's where the fish are bigger, stronger, toothier, and meaner. The salt is where adventure is large and danger is enhanced. The people who make their living as saltwater guides are different too, in many ways.

Geraghty is a guide working out of Port O Call Marina on the Gordon River in Naples, Florida. His water is as diverse as his clientele. Three-generation families and away-for-a-few-days rowdies, vacationing Americans, Germans, Italians, Brazilians, and Venezuelans, millionaires and wage earners, novices and veterans all have hired Captain Will to explore the fishing opportunities on the Naples-Marco region's tidal creeks, mangroves estuaries, flats, passes, and open Gulf of Mexico. Sharks, barracuda, grouper, permit, jacks, snook, redfish, tarpon, sheepshead, and many other species have flopped on the decks of his Grand Slam since he began his professional guiding in 1997.

He also writes the weekly fishing column in the *Naples Daily News*, a task that keeps him in close contact with other guides throughout his

A pelican snoozes on a dock on the Gordon River in Naples, Florida.

home region. His network augments his vast on-the-water experience, and the two combined to catch my attention when I wanted to know more about fishing Southwest Florida waters.

I paid him a visit one day. A three-day stubble dappled Captain Will's cheeks and chin, nearly matching the length of his close-cropped hair. As he worked on his boat at the dock, gulls screeched and pelicans snoozed. Boat traffic plied the Gordon River waters near the Tin City district. US 41 Tamiami Trail highway traffic clattered in the background as he talked with his visitor about life as a saltwater fishing guide and much more.

I had come to learn about the salt. I left with a new appreciation for the people who go to the water not only because they want to be there, but also because people are paying them good money.

Captain Will hadn't always been a guide. He was schooled at Naples High and Edison State College Collier Campus, and had an interest in a range of subjects, including anthropology. He hopped around from profession to profession, building houses for a while in New Jersey and assisting in the kitchen of a high-end restaurant in Naples. He learned a lot from cutting carrots and eventually worked his way up to a good position—"way over my head considering my cooking background."

His restaurant work started early, and by 2:00 p.m. he usually was back at his home on the water. He had a lot of time to fish from the skiff he kept tied behind his house. He loved fishing. His angling experience dated back to days he fished with his grandfather Norville McGowan. Grandpa McGowan chased bluefish and stripers around the tidewater near his home in Brooklyn, New York, then retired early to pitch baits for bass, play golf, and grow fruit trees, poinsettias, and roses near Lake Placid, Florida.

Captain Will's grandfather was a "sly perfectionist" who coached fishing with a critical mindset. "I might hook and boat a ten-pound largemouth bass, but then endure a stern lesson in what I'd done wrong during the battle," he said, twisting and turning in his chair, wielding an imaginary rod in reaction to the imaginary bass's lunges.

So he learned. He also learned while fishing the bountiful waters around Naples Pier. He credits the pier as a major reason he gained a solid foundation in fishing. "It was a melting pot of cultures, as well as an amazing fish-attracting structure," said Captain Will. "The pier's wooden pilings snagged decades and decades of ocean-tossed debris that created a wonderful reef-like environment for a diversity of species, including big grouper and tarpon."

The anglers who lugged their gear out on the pier were equally diverse. Captain Will recalls many of them by name and learned from all. Some he studied only by observation, as they were mum about their techniques. Others were grandfatherly types who always had advice to share. Still

Captain Will Geraghty at the helm of his Grand Slam in Naples, Florida.

others, especially the local Portuguese elders, earned considerable respect for their seemingly natural talents in fishing.

His youthful experiences served Geraghty well when he decided one day during his work in the restaurant kitchen to get a captain's license. He wanted to go about it without fanfare, but his buddy Al spilled the beans, and soon a Neapolitan who owned several boats asked newly certified Captain Will whether he'd skipper one of them for fishing clients. He learned the business as the boat owner's contractor, at the same time promoting and operating his own boat, the Grand Slam.

Patience is critical for the person who wants to succeed as a fishing guide. Captain Will works not only as a guide, but as a teacher, and the job can be trying, particularly when novices are aboard. Guides who scream at their anglers like they are at football practice soon will notice a decline in their bookings.

Captain Will has coped with all manner of circumstances among his clientele, from a huge range of skill and experience to language barriers to people who bring their "land-based issues" out on the Grand Slam.

It is critical, he said, to be patient with each individual and figure out how best to deliver what the client has paid for: to have fun.

Captain Will says he inherited a teacher's DNA from his father, who was a college professor and psychiatrist. It has helped him gauge each party and understand which portion of the Naples-area fishery is going to satisfy its "fun" quotient. That is particularly important with children, he noted, "because once you lose them it is very hard to rally the family."

Out on the water, anything can happen. The guide must work to make certain everybody is comfortable and trusting that the outcomes they desire will be achieved. Occasionally a guide will encounter a jackass who prefers to be rude, demanding, drunk, or all of the above. They are a challenge, and Captain Will has learned he must (and does) find a way to help them have fun.

Captain Will's Naples is an affluent area with outstanding weather and excellent fishing waters. Those factors combine to create a perfect environment for the saltwater guide and naturalist. He has pursued continuing education in ecology and combines fishing and environmental information to elevate his clients' awareness about the region's delicate balance. It makes his guests' outings all the more fulfilling.

The demands of a saltwater fishing guide's work are many. Captain Will noted his job is harder these days, considering the myriad of challenges. But he's quick to note a plumber could say the same thing about his work.

The workplace changes every day in the world of a saltwater fishing guide. The tides bring and the tides take. Sandbars move. Weather fronts barge in and linger like unwanted visitors. Bait migrates, and game species follow eons of instinct.

But back at the dock, the gulls still screech and the pelicans still snooze. At the end of the day, the rods stowed and the Grand Slam's deck rinsed, Captain Will drives home with the satisfaction that he's helped inform another group of people about the water and why they can love and appreciate it as much as he does.

CHAPTER 21

When the story must be told

Every week since 1988, I have sat down next to a keyboard and tapped out a five-hundred-to-six-hundred-word newspaper column. I did and still do that work not as an employee of the newspaper, but as a contributor paid on a per-piece basis.

Originally published on the outdoors-news page of *The Vindicator* in Youngstown, Ohio, my column today floats throughout the sports section of the *Tribune Chronicle* in Warren, Ohio, and in the sister edition named *Vindicator* after the *Trib*'s owners acquired that name when the *Vindy* ceased publishing in August 2019.

Writing the column has been a pleasure I could not even have imagined when I was a young man in college wondering what in the world I would end up doing with my life. One of the reasons I have loved doing the column is that I use fishing as the foundation for the stories I share. Another reason is the readers. They are front and center in my head every time I begin the process that ultimately results in that week's column. I literally write for them.

The joy is supreme. But so too is the obligation. Every week I must produce. There are no retreads. I have missed only a few weeks since 1988. Two of them were due to a space crunch imposed by the editor following particularly distressing economic news in our community. I write more about that experience in Chapter 41. The other missed column was because I was in the hospital following a heart attack. When I realized I was approaching deadline with an IV dripping nitroglycerin through the needle in my arm, I felt this overpowering doom—not because I was in a potentially life-ending predicament, but because the page editor would be irked as he looked for the missing column.

I recovered, of course, and resumed my weekly column writing. I am approaching the 1,700-column milestone. The commitment is relentless. Imagine you have a weekly task and must set aside an hour to dedicate to executing that task. You have no choice. You cannot brush it aside. It's got to be done. It's like the tide, arriving on schedule without interruption whether I am ready or not.

My task is made easier because I always begin with a root thought. Or, almost always. Most columns start and flow like the water from a spring—smooth and consistent. Some, however, take forever to develop and then seem to swirl like a backwater eddy that can't seem to find the main current.

Over the years, my column has ebbed and flowed around the subject of fishing. Sometimes it's about how to catch fish. But like the chapters in this book, my newspaper pieces are more stories that have fishing as their core rather than advice about lures and tactics. I believe we all have tales to tell to those who will listen, so the column has come to be my weekly podium for stories that must be told.

Much has happened in our world since my first newspaper fishing column. Presidents have come and gone. America has been attacked. Industries have flourished and foundered. Americans have become more prone to bicker with one another. A pandemic spread across the globe. Throughout it all, the column was written, published, and read.

Or so I think it is read. I imagine readers reading the column. It helps me write when I can visualize a reader being pulled in by the headline and lead. Sometimes readers send me emails with comments and questions. I appreciate their interest, so I have responded to every email, card, and letter (back in the days when people put pen to paper and wrote cards and letters).

People have asked me if I have a favorite column. I do not. I love having had the opportunity to write every one of them and believing that people seek and read them. Several stand apart from all of the others because they were especially personal to me. One was written for the Saturday following Tuesday, September 11, 2001. The other was the column that marked the resumption of my writing after my 2011 heart attack.

The hope of every writer is that readers are entertained or inspired, sometimes both. Writers want readers to feel what they feel. When I write for you, I want you to feel the sun, the rain, the thrill of a strike, and the joy of a successful day, regardless of the measure. I want you to see the glistening shower of water around a leaping fish, hear the line sizzle as it slices the surface over the run of a big fish, and smell the musty sweetness of a lowland swamp.

We have much to learn in more ways than one. My column may teach a little about fishing, but that rarely is my mission. Instead, my hope is readers will learn things that make their lives a little more interesting, perhaps even a bit more fulfilling, but always something that makes their world a little bit wider.

Events have a way of adding perspective, even for the fishing writer. In the wake of 9/11, my heart attack, and the COVID-19 pandemic, I found perspective in fishing—not to trivialize the serious ramifications, but to remind myself that whatever our circumstances and regardless of our preparedness, we must never take our lives for granted.

Think, for a moment, about what we do on the water. No matter how successful the previous one hundred casts might have been, we have no guarantee the one hundred and first will catch a fish. No matter how much experience we have driving our boat across the lake, we have no guarantee we'll get back to the dock today.

On the water, as it should be everywhere, all people are equal. We all have goals and dreams, talents and resources, and a primordial urge to connect with the life that swims in our rivers, lakes, and seas.

For these reasons and more, I will continue my newspaper column as long as an editor sees fit to permit me to entertain and inform.

CHAPTER 22

An angler of mythical proportions

Some people can paint a picture that stirs souls across centuries. Some can squarely hit a baseball traveling nearly 100 mph. Some can catch fish with such success that it seems they have bridged the human-piscatorial communication gap.

Rick Clunn is seventy-four years old as I write this chapter and approaching fifty years as a professional bass fisherman.

Over the span of five decades, he morphed from computer programmer to fishing guide to world champion to what many judge as the greatest of all time. His rise often seemed to be propelled more by sheer willpower than any special talent, secret tactic, or new technique.

Clunn won when the odds were against him. He won when others should have won. He won when some said he was done. And he won more often than 99 percent of the people against whom he competed.

I was in the boat one day when Clunn went fishing. It was during the world championship bass tournament, the Bass Masters Classic. It was in August on a sprawling reservoir in Alabama.

I was Clunn's observer that day, assigned to accompany him from start to finish for two reasons. The sanctioning agency, the Bass Anglers Sportsman Society, wisely added fishing writers to the tournament boats to gain news coverage to elevate the stature of the organization and competing professionals and to demonstrate to the world that the competition was fairly fought.

Clunn, of course, hardly needed any writer's copy to elevate his reputation. He was, by that time, known as the greatest of all time. And here I am, sitting two feet to the GOAT's port side, wondering at the wonder of my good fortune.

But there was a bit of a glitch as our day began. Lightning bolts ripped the dawn clouds, from which were falling sheets of rain during the morning takeoff. An Alabama August thunderstorm was in full form as the dock disappeared behind us.

I knew the stakes that day. I didn't expect Clunn to turn back. I knew he wouldn't run for shelter. And he didn't. Mile after mile of Alabama lake water passed under the boat as we rode through the rain at 65 mph. Sometimes it slowed. Sometimes it intensified. But it did not stop.

I ducked my head to hide my face from the stinging raindrops. Do you know what rain feels like on your forehead and cheeks at more than a mile a minute? Think needles. Millions of needles, nonstop, for half of an hour.

Occasionally I tilted my face toward Clunn and squinted to spy a clue that he was about to throttle back and start fishing. Nope. He didn't even flinch when lightning lit up the sky. I've fished in the rain and boated through some tricky weather. But I'd never been up for such a long haul in such miserable conditions.

On we went until finally the boat slowed. I started to feel we might actually survive the day. Clunn unbuckled his life jacket and slipped it off his shoulders as he jumped to the front deck with a casting rod locked and loaded. He began fishing without even a comment about the thrashing he'd just endured.

I, on the other hand, was not feeling so great. Our high-speed race through the cloudburst had gotten the best of my rainsuit. Gore-Tex or not, the fabric was beaten. Water had penetrated every seam, the zipper, and the hood. I was soaked to the bone and starting to shiver.

Clunn is known as a man who doesn't talk much when fishing. I can relate. It's all business out there, especially when it's a person's business.

So I didn't let him know I was in distress. Geesh. How do you tell the GOAT you think it might be a good idea to return to the dock? "Ya, I know you are competing for the world championship and a king's ransom in cash, but hey, whaddya say we go home early?"

I learned that day hypothermia is possible even in August in Alabama. The bone-chilling wind and rain did harm to my body, but I still had the wits to think about overcoming the distress. BASS had provided a cooler with sandwiches, cookies, fruit, and water. My brain recognized the need for calories, so I ate my lunch at seven in the morning. I think I may have eaten Clunn's lunch too, but he didn't notice.

The calories, meanwhile, lit the fire in my core, and with the help of the poststorm sunshine, I recovered to the point where I could observe the angler on the bow of the boat.

He was busy fishing. And catching. Soon he had a limit of largemouths and set to work to upgrade his weight with bigger bass to cull the smaller ones.

He spoke very little. He said "Let's go" when it was time to move to another location, and once he blurted an expletive when a nice-sized largemouth broke his spinnerbait and swam free.

Ours wasn't a verbal day, but I learned a lot. I saw confidence personified. He never seemed to waver or second-guess himself. He zigged when it was time to zig and zagged when it was time to zag.

He reminded me of other sports' GOATs. Ted Williams. Muhammad Ali. Tom Brady. Tiger Woods. You know their accomplishments are legendary, far beyond those of their peers, thanks to an almost-impossible degree of talent driven by virtually unshakable confidence.

To hit a baseball better than any human ever had, to outwit a strong man who is trying to crush your face, to drive a football team to unprecedented success, and to outplay every golfer on the planet year after year after year are accomplishments that do not happen because of luck.

Clunn has all of the mechanical skills of a good angler, but so do many others. He possesses the same technology that money can buy for you and me. He casts and catches with the same rods, reels, and lures you and I can buy from Bass Pro Shops.

But he's the GOAT—and ESPN has said it is so—largely because he has the ability to lock in on detail that everyone else is too busy to notice. He can focus even when the storm is churning. He can hear the cues when the world is noisy. And he has not let age be a limit, having won at the highest level twice past the age of seventy.

Clunn is known to tune out the clutter and tune in to nature like few other people. *Bassmaster Magazine*'s former editor Dave Precht knows Clunn well and once quoted him in a column, "You can't reach your full potential unless you're using all your senses as fully as you can. It's what makes us alive. When I'm eating, I try to really taste my food. When I'm reeling a spinnerbait, I try to really feel what it's running into."

Precht further quoted Clunn: "Fishing makes you in tune with everything. You suddenly sense humidity and warmth in the air, and you think, 'Man, they'll hit a buzzbait right now!' The greatest reward in fishing is that heightened sense of being alive."

If you fish, you know what Clunn means—and you can appreciate how one man can rise so high in a sport where so much can go wrong. While the rest of us are knocked around by the variables, Clunn reads, adjusts, and wins.

I've seen him in action and watched as his philosophy was put into play. After that day I rode in the boat with Clunn, I clearly understood why he's an angler of mythical proportions.

CHAPTER 23
Hemingway, Williams, and Boggs

Sometime during my high school years, I learned Ernest Hemingway was a fisherman. That was pretty cool. Around about that same time, I read in one of the big-time outdoors sports magazines that baseball Hall of Famer Ted Williams was as good at catching tarpon in Florida as at hitting baseballs at Fenway Park.

I loved books when I was young. I also loved baseball and played a lot. The kids in my neighborhood hacked a diamond out of a vacant corner of a farmer's pasture waiting for the contractor to expand his development. We picked sides and played for hours in the summer sun, then went home to change into our Little League uniforms for organized ball. Five hours or more we played many days and imagined ourselves at the plate in the bottom of the ninth with the World Series on the line.

When it was too dark or wet or cold for baseball, I could find entertainment with books. They put me in experiences I'd never imagined and took me to places I'd never explored. Along the way, I learned about Hemingway and discovered he found adventure in places I would someday love to see. Like the fighting chair of a big boat on the Gulf Stream with a blue marlin on the line. Like thigh deep in a cold Montana river casting flies to cutthroat trout.

Books about baseball were high on my reading list. Credit goes to Clair Bee's Chip Hilton, the fictional sports hero young boys like me imagined we would grow to be if we practiced hard and always did the right things for the right reasons. Chip did occasionally walk a batter or make an out at the plate, but he somehow always managed to win the big game.

To me, Ted Williams was the real-life Chip Hilton. He hit the ball hard and often. He was a winner. The only thing that would have made him a bigger star to me was if he had played for my beloved Cleveland Indians.

I recall magazine stories about Williams's adventures in the Florida Keys fishing for bonefish and tarpon and other species that were pretty exotic for a kid in Ohio. That the Splendid Splinter was a fisherman seemed pretty cool to me.

Many years after discovering Hemingway and Williams shared my passion for fishing, I had a special opportunity to talk fishing with another baseball slugger. I was at a table at a hotel bar in Birmingham, Alabama, with Wade Boggs not too many years after he concluded his Major League Baseball career with, among other teams, the New York Yankees and Boston Red Sox. At the high point of his career, Boggs was one of the most feared batters in all of baseball. Turns out he also knows a thing or two about bass fishing.

"There are a lot of similarities between baseball and professional bass fishing," Boggs told me as we waited for another round. "You take the average guy off the street and he might not even touch a 95 mph fastball. It's the same with pro bass anglers. They will absolutely fish you to death over the long haul. Compared to weekend anglers, these guys have more quickness, better reaction to bites, and keener knowledge about where to fish."

In 1999, Boggs hit a milestone achieved by few Major Leaguers when he smacked the three-thousandth hit of his career while playing for the Tampa Bay Devil Rays (today known simply as the Rays). For his accomplishment, the team presented him with a commemorative Ranger bass boat. Soon thereafter, he started to gain an insider's perspective about the challenges of competitive fishing. I met up with him in Birmingham in 2002 when we were fellow competitors in the Citgo Bass Masters Celebrity Tournament on Lay Lake. Boggs fished aboard the boat of pro angler Brent Chapman.

"I was really impressed with how his mind works," said the man who was known for outfoxing baseball's greatest pitchers. "Watching these guys perform at such a superior level is very impressive.

"The dedication of these guys is something weekend anglers really can't understand until they see it up close like we did this year."

Boggs's comments struck a chord. Dedication comes with passion and commitment. Boggs was dedicated. Williams was dedicated. Hemingway was dedicated. They—and others—achieved greatness because they were dedicated.

Few know just how much pure dedication played into their success. We see the result. Hall of Fame careers. Volumes of acclaimed literature. And lives well spent thanks to time on the water with rods, reels, lines, and lures.

D'Arcy Egan and Jack Wollitz share a love of fishing and a combined total of more than sixty-five years of newspaper column writing. Egan retired from *The Plain Dealer* in Cleveland.

CHAPTER 24

When anglers find their missions

The twenty-first century was but a week or two old when I got a telephone call that still is delivering dividends more than twenty years later.

The woman on the other end of the phone call said the local United Way office was thinking about holding a bass tournament as a fundraiser. She called me because a board member had suggested the newspaper's fishing columnist might be helpful. "I'm told," she said, "that you might know someone who could help us organize the tournament."

I did, of course, and volunteered myself for the job. It was an opportunity to not only engage the fishing community in work that raised money for the many organizations that rely on United Way support, but also to elevate awareness about the great needs that existed throughout our community.

What a decision that turned out to be. The tournament grew, and anglers looked forward to participating each year. I met superdedicated UW staffers and amazing volunteers. My decision to chair the tournament led me to gain appreciation for the fact that anglers can turn their passion into a mission of service.

The United Way Bass Classic, as it came to be known, also proved to be my introduction to a man whose mission takes a back seat to none. He is Harry Emmerling, a burly man with a teddy bear disposition and a heart as big as they come.

Harry lives in East Liverpool, Ohio, a community whose angler members proudly declare themselves river rats. He is a single dad who came to understand well that many children lack access to some of the things that help make life fun and interesting.

Harry reminds me of a friend who coached high school football for more than twenty years. My coach friend says he wishes more of his peers in the schools had embraced the fact that sports can give kids purpose and a sense of accomplishment that can be pivotal in their growth into productive adult lives.

Can fishing serve that same role for youngsters? Harry Emmerling believed it could, and he set out to see what he could do about it. He founded a group that would later be known as the Student Fishing League, with a handful of teens who had little or no idea about how to bait a hook, much less read water, cast a line, or detect a bite.

The Student Fishing League delivers opportunities for young people who want to learn about fishing.

Harry had found his mission. Even with the monumental task of raising teenage daughters, Harry knew he could do more. And more is what he has done.

I met Harry several years ago through my efforts to differentiate our annual United Way Bass Classic from all of the hundreds of other bass tournaments on the lakes in Northeast Ohio and Western Pennsylvania. I was impressed by the "no limits" approach of the Major League Fishing competition format. MLF counts every bass a competitor catches, compared with tournament scoring formats that count only the angler's five largest bass. I wanted our United Way Bass Classic to count every bass caught by the anglers fishing the bass-filled waters of Evans and Pine lakes. They are reservoirs owned by water utility Aqua Ohio south of Youngstown.

But I had a problem. Not that we suspected anglers might exaggerate in scoring their fish, but we did need to make sure the competition was fair and square, above reproach. The two anglers on each tournament boat might combine to catch twenty or more bass, a total that simply cannot be kept alive and in condition to be released after the competition. Major League Fishing's format called for the catch to be immediately weighed and released, then having that weight recorded on a real-time online scoreboard.

That meant I needed to put a scorekeeper on every boat. Our tournament typically has more than sixty boats. I needed someone to sit aboard each boat and watch two people fish for seven hours. The observers—we called them judges—were to weigh and record each bass. I begged, coaxed, and cajoled forty friends, relatives, and strangers into volunteering as judges, but needed twenty-five more.

An Aqua Ohio employee told me he knew of Harry Emmerling's group of student anglers because he'd arranged for them to fish on Aqua waters. I hadn't yet heard about Harry and his Student Fishing League, so I called to see whether he might be able to help us recruit judges.

Without hesitation, Harry said, "No problem."

Not only does Harry assist kids in becoming familiar with fishing through the Student Fishing League, he also organizes activities that result in quantities of rods, reels, lures, and other fishing accessories for students who do not have the means to buy equipment. He also has a network of parents and advisers who chip in time and talents to instill appreciation and service attitudes among the student anglers.

Could the young anglers stand authoritatively enough in front of adult competitors who would insist on swift and accurate scoring? "No problem," Harry said.

Harry Emmerling and daughter at the Muransky Companies Bass Classic, where his Student Fishing League members worked as volunteer judges.

Indeed, it was no problem. In fact, our first year with teen anglers volunteering as judges was a huge success. The students helped us include a judge on all sixty-five competition boats and enabled our no-limits tournament to set an Ohio record for the single heaviest one-day-tournament winning catch of more than sixty-six pounds.

The next year, Harry again said "no problem." And the next year after that and every year thereafter, Harry smiles and asks, "How many judges do you need?"

Harry loves fishing as much as any other angler. But it would be a fair bet to wager he loves the mission of the Student Fishing League even more than fishing itself. He works twelve months a year in organizing events, recruiting boater coaches, coaxing moms into bringing food to the kids' outings, and even orchestrating the collection of a large selection of usable fishing equipment from which students can shop during the Christmas season.

When it comes to kids and fishing, Harry sees no obstacle as too much to overcome.

"No problem," says the man who found and followed his true fishing mission.

CHAPTER 25

On the water with big game hunters

A special tribe of anglers has grown as fishing morphed from subsistence to sport. Its members are known to have an almost primordial interest in pursuing fish that are at the pinnacle of the food chain, creatures that can eat just about every other species in their environment without much fear of becoming a meal themselves.

While they are scattered across the planet in ecosystems that don't always share the same species, the tribe's people are driven to fish for creatures with big bodies, dagger teeth, and alpha-predator dispositions. In the Amazon, they fish for arapaima. In Asia, they seek kaluga sturgeon. In Africa, they fish for Nile perch.

In America, they fish for muskellunge.

More popularly known by their clipped name, muskies are the apex fish in most North American waters. Their range extends from southern Canada to below the Mason-Dixon Line. They are genetically predisposed to do well in a variety of habitats. They thrive in natural lakes in Canada and the northern US, in small and large river systems, and in dammed impoundments.

What's as important as where muskies live is the spell they cast over people who have caught them. Are muskie fishers born? Perhaps some. But I believe those who come to call themselves "muskie angler" are converts. They joined the tribe after discovering an insatiable instinct to eschew lesser fish, those that might be relatively easy to catch, in favor of fish that are literally capable of scaring the bejabbers out of them and even hurting them.

Muskies do all of that and more. Long before I ever caught a muskie, I read the stories in *Outdoor Life* and *Field & Stream* about the fabled muskie sportfishing pioneers on legendary waters. I learned about the world record and a plethora of other yarns about the "fish of a thousand casts."

Then I met Chris DePaola.

Chris is a salesman by profession, but an angler at heart. He's retired now and can fish as often as he likes for muskies. One can argue, of course, that Chris fished for muskies as often as he liked even while working to keep his territory well supplied with Nestlé products.

Chris is a muskie angler's muskie fisherman. He's a man others reach out to when they want to know where they are biting and what they are hitting. He's hosted angling celebrities, including iconic muskie maniac Pete Maina and TV fishing funnyman Mark Zona.

Chris DePaola hunts and hooks giant muskies all across North America.

Virtually every lake in the US that is famous for muskie fishing is checked off Chris's list of been-there-done-that venues. He's lacking literally nothing when it comes to rods, reels, lures, boats, and knowledge especially dedicated to locating, casting, hooking, and boating monster muskies.

Before I met Chris, I had the opportunity to learn about muskies from Max Case. Max and Chris live not far from each other and are without question card-carrying members of the muskie fishing tribe.

I came to know Max as I was doing research for a magazine article about muskie fishing on Berlin Reservoir, a small lake on the Mahoning River halfway between Akron and Youngstown, Ohio. Word had filtered to me that Max had just recently hooked nine muskies during a Berlin fishing trip and boated seven of them. So much for "fish of a thousand casts."

Max and I scheduled a trip for photos. He did not disappoint. Not long after we launched the boat and he settled on the lures to drag for the day, Max hooked up with a rollicking muskie measuring forty-two inches. He carefully unhooked the trebles snagged in the fish's mouth and, with a gentle touch, glided the fish so that oxygen-laden water passed over its gills. With his nursing, the exhausted monster revived and swam out of view.

It was easy to understand how muskie fishing can get in your blood.

Fast-forward twenty years and Chris DePaola is on the phone, relating stories about fifty-inchers caught and released on great muskie waters Lake Saint Clair, Chautauqua, and Pymatuning. He talks about the thrills he has experienced, but is equally as delighted to spin tales about the successes of those who have shared his boat.

I have fished with Chris, but not for muskies. He took me one day to one of his favorite steelhead streams, near Lake Erie, and generously provided the exact setup required to catch a steelhead. It worked, but not because I was an expert. It worked because Chris was so meticulous in rigging the rod, reel, and lure and so specific in his instructions.

His knowledge of apex predators like steelhead and muskies is considerable. He is equally adept with either species. But I suspect steelhead are simply diversions for Chris to stay in practice and pass the time until cold weather wanes and the next muskie season is at hand.

Chris's passion for big game fishing is second to none. So is his delight in sharing what he knows so that others can experience the thrills he has enjoyed. I think people like Chris are among the reasons the worldwide tribe of big-fish fishers is so special.

Muskies like this one are prized for their sporting value.

CHAPTER 26

A wizard in walleye world

Some call him The Bull. I can see that. He's a big enough dude with a confident outlook that virtually shouts "don't get in my way."

He's Sammy Cappelli, aka The Bull, but I see him more as a wizard. He's a wizard in the world of walleye fishing.

Sammy was born to be an angler. In fact, he could have become a bass nut, because his father loved to fish for them. He recalls his youthful days drifting night crawlers on tiny hooks into likely bass holes in a little stream that drained into Berlin Reservoir, twenty-five miles from his home near Youngstown, Ohio.

Fishing was important to young Sammy, but football was more so—until a fateful day when, after playing two years for Cardinal Mooney High School, he skipped practice to go fishing at Lake Newport in Mill Creek Park.

That decision cost him not only his spot on the football team, but also a state championship ring. He regretted his mistake. It left a void in his life he vowed to fill.

By 2017, Sammy had become an accomplished walleye angler. He succeeded on the tougher-than-tough waters around home in Northeast Ohio, where walleyes see heavy fishing pressure from thousands of anglers who favor them for their superior table qualities. Generations of people have their favorite walleye recipes for family fish fries and holiday celebrations. For much of the modern era of fishing around Youngstown, few walleyes ever escaped the hot grease in cast-iron frying pans.

Tournament angling popularized catch-and-release fishing for bass and walleyes in the 1980s and '90s, resulting in increasing numbers of fish of both species being released to be caught again. Walleye fishing got better even as anglers became more sophisticated in their tactics.

Sammy was a member of the wave of competition anglers specializing in the walleyes in their hometown waters. He won often as he mastered the techniques of anglers from far-flung walleye waters as they became publicized in magazine articles and YouTube videos. Soon he ventured out from local success and fished in tournaments throughout the Upper Midwest.

In 2017, Sammy and tournament partner Erick Williams earned a berth in the Cabela's National Walleye Team Championship. From an estimated 165,000 teams throughout the United States, Sammy and Erick were among the select 251 teams to gain invitations to the national championship. They were understandably jazzed about the opportunity, especially the fact that it was on water they knew very well: Lake Erie.

They scouted thoroughly and practiced hard and began the first of three days of competition with a positive attitude. The work paid off, and they were ninth after day one. Day two went equally well; Sammy and Erick were third overall, well within striking distance for the national title. They concluded their third day with a ten-pound Erie giant. When the scales dried after day three, Sammy and his teammate tallied fifteen walleyes weighing 107.3 pounds. They were national champs, with a pair of big new boats, thousands of dollars in cash and merchandise, and gleaming trophies.

But for Sammy, the title also was vindication of his decision to skip that day of football practice. Along with the national title came a champion's ring. "I wanted that ring more than the boats and the money," he said. "I wanted that ring to give to Dad. All I ever wanted to do was win a championship ring to give to him."

Even with a national championship on his résumé, Sammy does not underestimate the importance of continuous learning and refining. Expanding his fishing horizons has always been important. He said he thought he was a pretty good fisherman until he started tournament fishing. He soon learned that if he was going to call himself a professional, he needed to learn how to catch them not just on the good days, but on bad days too.

"The tournaments where I learn the most are those when I did the worst," he said. "I tell people, 'Don't listen to dock talk.' I fish what I've learned, not by trying to duplicate what others are doing."

Sammy has accomplished a lot in the walleye world, but what if he'd never become a competition angler?

"I would have been a teacher," said The Bull. "I love sharing what I know. After we won the national championship, I only fished three times that year. When you set a goal that high and achieve it, you can't top it."

Today he enjoys any and all opportunities to teach children and adults. He does fishing instruction programs at schools near his home and schedules ten or more outdoor-show teaching appearances annually.

"I love to give back. I really enjoy taking people out on the water and showing them how to catch fish."

What about "The Bull"? It was a nickname given by his friend Keith Walters. "I was a hothead when I was a kid. Stubborn, you know. And in football, if I hit you, you knew you'd been hit."

Walleye wizard Sammy Cappelli is a national champion who loves to teach others about fishing.

If The Bull sounds tough, consider the tournament he fished with a separated shoulder and detached bicep. Hurts even thinking about that, right? He suffered the injury after jumping from his boat to a rain-slick boat dock. He spent most of the night in a hospital ER, only to get out in the morning in time to make the launch of the first day of a three-day walleye tournament—with a separated shoulder and his bicep ripped from the bone.

Sammy has been on top of the mountain and relished the view. He's not done, by any stretch, but is satisfied with where he is today.

"If I never cash another check, I don't care. I've won a national championship. I'm not ready to stop, but when that time comes, I'll know it." He will borrow a page from his friend Joe Thomas, who retired after a career at left tackle for the Cleveland Browns that is likely to earn him a bust in the Pro Football Hall of Fame. "When it's time to hang 'em up, I'll just stop."

That day can't come soon enough for the walleyes, an untold number of which have flopped in Sammy's net. They knew when they had been hit by The Bull.

CHAPTER 27

My favorite place to fish

It is impossible to pick one place that I can unequivocally declare as my favorite place to fish. I can tell you my least favorite lakes, without hesitation, but zeroing in on the top three is pretty tough.

I am not exactly certain why a clear favorite hasn't emerged. I suppose it has to do with the variables. But there are many variables in other areas of my life, and yet I still can tell you what I like best within them.

So my favorite place to fish depends on the season, the weather, the species, the convenience, and even my mood. Some are favorites because they are pretty places. Some qualify because they are fish factories. Some have super facilities for anglers. Some present particular challenges. Some are private; most are public.

Some have a little of everything.

For example, I love Lake Erie. But I also know it can be a miserable place. You can catch a limit of several species of fish quickly—or you can go home skunked. You can have the most beautiful lake vistas, rocky islands, picturesque skylines—and you can be reduced to a vomiting wretch in seven-foot seas that can flip a boat like it was a bathtub toy.

Season? I love the spring, but summer and fall are pretty good too. Some of my most memorable fishing trips have happened on a frozen lake when the daytime high barely hit twenty degrees.

I have had loads of fun on a big lake three hours from home, but have had banner days on a little lake three minutes from my driveway. I bask in the glory of a sunny day on the lake, but have loved every minute of a rainy day of fishing.

I like to think my favorite lake is the one I am fishing. This helps me get into the right frame of mind, and being in the right frame of mind is as important to success in fishing as it is to success on the job, cooking dinner, playing golf, or whatever.

If forced to make a choice about my favorite place to fish, I would first make a list. It would include two well-known locales: Lake Erie and the Ohio River. They are about as opposite as two waterways might be, but we'll talk about that another time. The list also would include a pretty fishery in Western New York, Chautauqua. Also on my list are two reservoirs local to my home, Mosquito and Shenango. Don't ask me why I like a lake named after an annoying, stinging, disease-carrying insect, I just do. My list also would include waters far from home: Chickamauga, Okeechobee, Burt, Mullet, the Louisiana delta, and several others. I also would have to list the ponds around the golf course where we live a few months every year in Naples, Florida.

None are the same. In fact, they are similar only in that they are wet. But each at one time or another very well deserves to be called my favorite place to fish.

That is because I look forward to each and every opportunity to visit them with great anticipation. The lakes I listed above qualify under that criterion. I cannot think of even one instance when, considering the prospect of fishing there, I have ever thought, "Ugh. Why the hell am I going there tomorrow?"

My favorite lakes have more than once exceeded my wildest expectations.

Lake Erie is the walleye capital of the world, a world-class smallmouth bass fishery and home to a supercatchable population of exotic and acrobatic steelhead trout. I have enjoyed days when I literally caught them to the point where I felt I'd had enough fun for that trip.

It would stand to reason, therefore, that Erie might be my favorite place to fish.

Before you guess Erie is that place, consider my case for the Ohio River. For sure, the river is known more as a servant of industry and barge commerce than as a "favorite" fishery. Its reputation among America's bass anglers ranges somewhere between sewer and sediment lagoon. But a select few river rats have experienced the Ohio River at its finest. When it's right, the river is really awesome. I have been on the receiving end of some of the finest smallmouth fishing imaginable. Fifty-fish days? Yes, and then some.

That is not to say the river is without challenges. Truth is, the Ohio River presents more challenges than just about any other lake or river I know. If opportunities to beat the odds, to solve a puzzle, to experience remarkable success are criteria for qualifications as a favorite place to fish, then I nominate the mighty Ohio.

But it's not that simple.

One would think the author's favorite place to fish is where he caught these beautiful bass.

Mosquito Lake near my home in Ohio is a fun place to fish. Consider this: I can catch a limit of walleyes in a few hours in the morning and add some slab-sided crappies, then spend the balance of the day hooking up with feisty largemouth bass. For a very modest investment of time and gasoline, I can have all that fun and still be home in time to fillet the walleyes and crappies for dinner. The lake is a paradise for anglers who fish for sport and for meat. They should call it Paradise Lake, which would seem a lot more chamber of commerce friendly than Mosquito. But we are fishing, not marketing, and Mosquito qualifies as one of my faves.

I have fished in nearly one hundred locations around the United States. An inlet in Maine, a beach on the Outer Banks, a bayou near New Orleans, the Big O in Florida, and a dozen or more reservoirs sprawled across the South. I have family-vacation fishing memories from the Northwoods of Michigan and fishing-buddy excursions on the Great Lakes. I have wet-waded creeks with mudbanks where Native Americans also left footprints. I have stood waist-deep in waders with cold water trying to sweep me off my feet while casting for walleyes, white bass, and steelhead trout. I have spent countless days on my boat on Ohio, Pennsylvania, and New York lakes where every day is a new challenge in beautiful and familiar scenery surrounding waters I know like the back of my hand. Is there a favorite among them? Maybe, but then I can think of a hundred reasons why others might be a favorite too.

And as I write this sentence, I am sitting with a view of a spot where just three weeks ago I caught a five-pound largemouth bass on my very first cast, with a dewy pink sunrise as the backdrop. Such a spot, with easy pickings, might very well be my favorite place to fish.

Decisions, decisions. So many choices. You've read my clues. Have you determined my favorite place to fish? No? Neither have I.

So I guess when it's all said and done, my favorite place to fish is among the memories in my mind. Without them, I'm pretty much foundering.

CHAPTER 28

Greeting the sun

If there is a better place on earth than a calm lake at sunrise, I haven't yet seen it.

No painting is prettier. No poem is more inspiring. No sculpture is more meaningful. Dawn over a waterscape is the perfect earthly reminder that fresh starts are available to all of us all of the time. We just need to go get them.

I've been launching boats and driving out to fishing holes at dawn for most of my life. I cannot even guess how many sunrises I have witnessed. But I can darn sure tell you that while fishing during each and every sunrise, I have never, ever felt even a twinge of regret about where I was and what I was doing.

The start of each day is a blessing for all, but I can think of few activities for which that start is more symbolic than fishing. As the world awakens, the well-prepared angler is poised to seize the day. Carpe diem indeed.

Sunrise means the slate is clean. Yesterday's mistakes are erased, but so are our successes. It is good to have the mistakes in our past and forget them. It also is good to have the accomplishments in the rearview mirror, where we can sneak a peek for inspiration.

I think it is fitting that the sunrise palette is vivid but soft. It is pastel pink that knows exactly when to blush to blaze orange, gray that saunters to lavender, and mauve that morphs to cherry red.

Sunrise reminds us the world can refresh. Earth handles a lot of abuse, and each fresh dawn reminds us our planet can forgive us if we stop messing with it.

For anglers, sunrise also means the fish are hungry. Many species of fish rely on their sight to hunt and capture food, so the new day's first light gives predators an advantage they lacked during the previous ten hours.

I just flat-out love getting to the lake just as the eastern horizon starts to glow. The air is cool and fresh, perfect for the get-ready chores necessary to set up the boat for the day's action. By the time I am ready, the light is good for a quick run to the first stop of the morning.

Fishing days start with the kind of promise a beautiful sunrise delivers. I usually pick up the topwater rod first, with high hopes the bass are looking to the surface for shad and perch, a frog or a snake, perhaps even a little bird or rodent. Any or all of them might be on the surface of a lake as the sun breaks over the treetops.

I have watched the sun rise over the Atlantic in Maine, Massachusetts, Maryland, Virginia, and the Carolinas. I've seen it rise over lakes Michigan and Erie, and rivers and impoundments in Ohio, Pennsylvania, New York, Kentucky, Virginia, Tennessee, Arkansas, Alabama, Louisiana, and Florida. It is always special, especially with rod in hand and the fish in an eating mood.

Given a choice, I would schedule most every fishing trip to coincide with the sun's return to the lake of my day. I'm a confident angler regardless of the conditions, but who can argue with the boost we get from a dramatic dawn?

Sunrise fails us in at least one measure, and that is that it is so fleeting. But I suppose if the sunrise lingered, we would take it for granted—and a good lesson I've learned during a lifetime on the water is we must never take anything for granted.

If there is a better time to be on the water than sunrise, I've not yet experienced it.

Dawn over a waterscape is the perfect reminder that fresh starts are
available to all.

CHAPTER 29

Bump in the night

The sun rises. The sun sets. So go the days of our planet. That is the natural order for life on earth.

But for a few, the sun sets and then it rises. Their day is in darkness. They are the ones who fish all night. Theirs is a world where most anglers, even the most ardent, do not bother to venture.

But it also is a world well worth visiting by those who are looking for new dimensions in their own pursuit of fishing satisfaction.

We all have experienced the night. An after-dinner stroll around the neighborhood, the drive home after a date, Halloween trick-or-treating, a football game under the lights—all after-dark activities that extend our daily hours of fun.

Most after-dark activity is relatively brief and concludes at a reasonable hour when bedtime beckons. Humans are creatures who depend so much on seeing that we reserve the darkness for resting.

The night also is a time when other animals perk up. They may lay low during the day and hunt for food when the cover of darkness makes stalking prey more likely to succeed. Such is the case with the night fisher.

Something very different happens in the head of an angler launching a boat in the twilight. It's kind of against our grain. Typically I lay out rods and reels for a morning flurry with the notion that I'll soon stow them in favor of rods better suited for presenting lures to grind out bites as the day advances.

A night fishing trip is different. Anglers must be ready for the flurry hours after sunset and geared up with tackle that doesn't require visual acuity to execute.

But that's just the tip of the iceberg. Vision is reduced, but your hearing is enhanced. A raccoon splashing at the water's side may echo like an alligator on the attack. A bat may swoosh past your face and you'll swear it was an F-16.

About those bats: their radar helps them locate tiny insects in inky blackness. The same sensory organ also tricks them into thinking our thin strands of fishing line are buggy meals. Bats ticking the fishing line cause touchy anglers to jerk back against phantom "bites."

Bats aren't the only things bumping in the night.

Until you have had a three-pound smallmouth bass freight-train your spinnerbait on a dark night, you really haven't felt a vicious strike. Even the throb of the oversized Colorado blade on a nighttime spinnerbait is a sensation with which daytime-only fishers are not familiar. The most effective blades are deep-cupped rounds stamped from steel and lacquered black. They are about the size of a silver dollar and thump and bump on every rotation as the angler cranks the spinnerbait back to the boat. The vibration transmits up the line, through the rod's reel seat, into the angler's hand and arm.

Our senses of hearing and touch are on high alert during night fishing trips, as is the all-important ability to perceive and calculate the distance to casting targets in the enveloping gloom. A bright moon may provide a bit of light on clear nights, but that is hardly enough to let the angler know whether the cast will land in the rocks of a riprap bank or kiss the water the perfect two feet from the shore.

As the hours of darkness advance, human eyesight adjusts. The sights impossible to see just after sunset gradually become apparent as the clock ticks on. We see deer sipping from the bank, otters and minks chasing through the leaves, a fox loping across a meadow, and even a bass boil the surface as it chases a shad pinned against the lake's shore.

A bass hooked during the day is difficult enough to corral. A bass that has crashed the lure at night is twice the challenge. You often will hear the fish before you see it, as it cartwheels out in the murky distance. Once the battle is cranked close to the boat, the fun becomes sensing where exactly the fish is relative to the boat and the surface.

A misconception about night fishing is that it is better than daytime. That's not always the case. The dusky hours are productive, but anglers frequently experience a decided lull as full darkness comes. The best fishing, in my experience, often is after midnight. I suspect it has something to do with fish's own vision, and how they use the minimal light to their advantage in silhouetting prey against the surface.

An all-nighter is perhaps the best incarnation of the reality of time. All abstractness is removed for the person who witnesses the sunset, then lives with all senses sharply tuned through the dark hours, and finally sees the black over the treetops transition to gray and pink.

When you finish your fishing trip with the sunrise lighting the boat ramp, you appreciate the roundness of our world. The cycle of time is complete as you fill in the experience you miss when you live only from dawn to dark. And, if you were lucky enough, you also caught a few fish to make the time even more well spent.

CHAPTER 30

What would Izaak Walton say?

In his angling epic, *The Compleat Angler*, Izaak Walton wrote prose and poetry to describe idyllic meadow streams where fishers cast tiny flies to trout whose gills had never filtered anything but the purest of cold spring water.

Walton wrote in London well before the Industrial Revolution. While the Thames River was fouled by human exploitation for centuries before the first belching factories, the countryside streams were where people went with fly rod in hand. Sheep or cattle may have contributed a little to the waters' organic load, but not so much as to be considered polluted.

Writer Walton could not possibly have conceived of a day when people would angle in waters that flowed through valleys lined with industry and whose residents numbered in the tens of millions. He could not have foreseen steel mills, coal-fired power plants, nuclear reactors, petrochemical processing complexes, refineries, and other effluent-expelling operations.

So Walton set his story in pristine surroundings where spring-fed brooks swelled to rivers that flowed to lakes that drained to the sea without picking up much to make them undrinkable. "Idyllic" is the word.

But idyllic certainly is in the eye of the beholder. Disagree? Consider two rivers where I often fish: the Ohio and the Mahoning.

When I was a young boy, the people of Youngstown, Warren, Niles, Girard, Struthers, Campbell, and Lowellville dismissed the Mahoning River as a waterway so polluted that nobody considered fishing there.

While the Mahoning rose from a spring in a pasture and swelled from brook to creek to river, it would never be mistaken for a limestone creek in seventeenth-century England. Nonetheless, I find it to be idyllic in many ways.

During the years that I worked in downtown Warren, I found numerous opportunities to enjoy what I termed a "no calorie lunch." That is, I drove over to a nearby park, loosened my tie, and pulled out a casting rod to which I had tied a tandem willow leaf spinnerbait in hopes of catching a few Mahoning River smallmouth bass.

The banks of the river were tree-lined and tranquil. The sycamores and oaks muffled the street noise and urban clatter. The shore near the water was muddy enough that I needed to clean my loafers before trudging back into my office when the lunch break was over. Once in a while I slipped and got a wet leg. I carried a rag to wipe fish slime off my hands, but coworkers no doubt could catch a whiff if the fishing hour had been productive.

With steel mills and power plants, the Ohio River is not exactly Izaak Walton's idyllic River Lea. But the author finds the Ohio can indeed be idyllic.

Such an idyllic lunch break. For sixty minutes (OK, sometimes seventy), I was out of touch of phones, emails, deadlines, meetings, and worries. It was me, the river, and, often, a few fish. It wasn't paradise, but how close can one expect to get to that when the workaday world is bare minutes away?

Many years after I left Warren and my no-calorie lunches, I was invited to go on a kayak float on the lower Mahoning with a friend, Tim Brown, who specializes in river smallmouth bass. We put in at a bridge and paddled seven or eight miles, fishing riffles and eddies that yielded dozens of spunky bass. Just a few miles from shorelines lined with shuttered factories, railroad switchyards, and municipal sewage treatment plants, the river ran clear, and lush waterside vegetation grew thick and green. Hardwood trees topped out in a shady canopy, and we spied a bald eagle perched like the king of the river, surveying his domain for the slightest hint of a fish, a rodent, or a reptile. Two deer sipped as we rounded a bend, and an owl glided on silent wings a hundred yards beyond our boats.

I cannot imagine a more idyllic afternoon for an angler just fifteen minutes from his home in suburban Ohio. The only hints of civilization were the highway bridges under which we passed, but we hardly noticed. Who cared, with eagles and deer and smallmouth bass around us?

I have never seen Walton's River Lea, but it would seem to be the picture of idyllic. It is surmised Walton went there to escape from the hubbub of London and the conflicts of the day in 1650s England. Three hundred and seventy years later, I can relate.

We all need a place where the world doesn't much matter, where the only concerns are the next drink of water, the vista around the bend, and the next fish to strike our lure.

It seems silly then to compare the River Lea to the Ohio River. But like my Mahoning, the Ohio is a place where I can be by myself in a sea of people with industrial clatter on the hillsides rising from the water and maritime commerce churning the waters.

The Ohio is not the fishiest water I know. Its reputation, in fact, has been sullied by poor results by the world's best bass anglers competing in major professional championship tournaments. But I love the place. The pool closest to home is but a bare three-quarters-of-an-hour drive from my house, so I go there often enough to call it home water.

It doesn't always play fair, of course, but what lake or river does? I have on occasion returned home with nothing more than an empty gas tank and a sunburn. But the challenge is welcome, as the days when an angler figures out the puzzle are the best days to be had. When the Ohio is good to me, it's very, very good.

Add all the other cool nature stuff to what I know about the Ohio River. It's got bald eagles, lots of them, turkeys on the hillsides, otters and minks darting and dodging on the giant boulders that have tumbled off steep slopes, deer swimming from Ohio to West Virginia and vice versa, and a whole bunch more that keen eyes might see.

The Ohio is a challenging place where nature perseveres. It's kind of like the people who call the Ohio Valley home. Fun and resilient. That's why I love it.

It may not be yours, but it is my version of idyllic.

Walton wrote, "As no man is born an artist, so no man is born an angler." And I'm telling you that as rivers are not necessarily born perfect, any of them can be a man's perfect place.

Kayak angler Tim Brown finds great joy in paddling and casting for smallmouth bass on the Mahoning River in northeastern Ohio.

CHAPTER 31

Waist-deep in ice water (and other things to fear)

The rush of the cold water compressed the neoprene leggings around my ankles and calves, then my knees and thighs as I inched deeper across the slick stones that formed the bottom of the river I had selected that March morning for a few hours of bouncing jigs for walleyes.

Frost on tree twigs hanging over the river glistened as the sun cleared the ridge to my east and lent energy to the morning. It would be a mild day, a little ahead of the season, the perfect conditions to activate a rush of walleyes toward the gravel shoals where they would seek to spawn.

It was the kind of day when an angler cannot resist the urge to go to the water, rod and reel in hand, to test talents versus the fish's instinctual behavior.

I stepped carefully in the river, moving to a position where I could cast my jig and guide it over a spot likely to hold prespawn walleyes. My chest-high waders kept my feet, legs, and butt dry, but were not much of a barrier for the chill that the current pushed through the rubber into my skin, meat, and bones. At forty degrees, the water was decidedly cold enough to make me appreciate the insulation I'd donned before pulling on the waders.

Wading anglers know the risks of stepping off dry land into the water, where hazards are never more than a misstep away. But as in many other areas of life, we do our risk-reward analysis, and we decide whether it's worth stepping out. Risks abound in the world of fishing. Danger lurks on and in the water, whether we're on foot or in a canoe, kayak, bass boat, or forty-eight-foot Hatteras. We make the plunge, so to speak, with a healthy dose of fear.

I have to admit, however, that standing waist-deep in ice water is chilling—not only in temperature. It can send shivers up an angler's spine.

Consider the threats. Unless the water is as clear as James Bond's martini, the angler cannot see his or her feet. Will the next step be into a hole deeper than the angler's chin? Your brain knows there are rocks out there that pose trip hazards. Will your toe know when one is near? The moss on the rocks can be as slick as rink ice after the Zamboni's work is done.

Never underestimate the force of the current. An angler who has an issue with equilibrium would be wise to forgo wading. The movement of the water alone can confuse the senses; fluctuations in the force can literally sweep the feet away.

It happened to me. Coho salmon were in the rivers that run into Lake Erie. It was December, and a trace of snow lined the riverbank where I planned to fish. Dressed in layers of insulated underwear and flannel, I pulled on my waders, laced up my felt-soled wading shoes, and trudged over to the river with spinning rod in hand. With caution, I stepped into the water and worked my way to a pool where I hoped salmon were holding. Thirty minutes of casting produced no strikes, so I turned to retrace my steps to the bank, where I could make quick work of finding the next likely fishing hole.

Before I got to the bank, however, the water literally pushed me off my feet. It was only knee-deep, but the water's force caught me at just the right moment, as my next step landed awkwardly. I landed on my butt, and the current caught me broadside, sliding me downstream feetfirst, which was a problem because the air trapped in my waders converted my feet into floats. After about twenty or thirty feet of riding the riffle, I finally grounded. I clamored to my feet and came to the realization that my hooded sweatshirt was soaked like a sponge on car-wash day. The belt I'd cinched around my waders at my waist kept the water from flowing down to my legs. By the time I got back to my van, my cotton sweatshirt was frozen solid around my shoulders and neck.

It could have been worse, of course, but my day was done.

I am not an expert on all of the fears we anglers harbor, but I have experienced a few dangerous situations personally. Anything can happen. That's one of the lessons instructors of boating-safety classes pound into their students' minds. I took a Power Squadron class many years ago. I don't remember all of the points the instructor made, but I do remember him pointing out that boats don't have brakes and that when navigating upstream, the skipper must remember "red right returning."

We take precautions, but we know there will be accidents. Two of mine are still vivid in my mind even though many years have passed since they happened.

After a June rainstorm subsided and the sun broke through the murky sky over the Ohio River, the summer mugginess became more than I cared to endure under my black rainsuit. I went to the back deck of friend Steve Zarbaugh's boat, peeled off the jacket, and stood on one leg to free my foot from the pants. Bad decision. The boat rocked, I lost my balance, fell to my knees, and rolled into the river. The current pulled me away from the boat, but my friend was quick to recognize my peril. I still can see the concern in his eyes as he extended his arm so that I could grab his hand. Steve is a strong man, and he pulled me to the deck, where I flopped like a catfish. Our combined adrenaline made short work of the rescue, but we both were a bit shaken over the mishap.

Truth be told, I've fallen overboard two other times. I could tell you about the missteps that caused both incidents, but you get the picture.

Another fear for those of us who operate boats is the possibility of launching with the drain plug not secure or missing altogether. We can laugh about the times we have seen missing-plug incidents at boat ramps. Less funny, of course, are the times when the plug somehow pops out of its hole in the transom when the boat is far from the dock.

It happened to wife Barb and me one April afternoon on a lake near our home. It was a nice spring day and crappies were biting, so we hitched up the boat. Launching went smoothly, and we motored a mile or so to a spot where we dropped anchor, tossed out hooks baited with minnows, and sat back to watch our floats dance on the ripples. The sun was out, the red-winged blackbirds were trilling, and we had lunch in the cooler. The afternoon promised to be quite pleasant.

After only a minute of our idyllic outing, Barb noticed the carpet under our feet was soggy. I splashed back to inspect the bilge, which was completely flooded. The water was rising and the boat was, well, sinking. I pulled the anchor, started the outboard, and pushed the gear shifter to forward. The engine labored to push our waterlogged vessel to plane, but as we gained speed, the siphoning action of the water at the transom sucked the bilge dry. We made it to the dock, and Barb kept the boat moving in a circle as I backed the trailer in for loading.

The drain plug that seemed so secure during prelaunch inspection had popped out. The carpet was wet and we were embarrassed, but we had survived one of boaters' worst fears.

Danger lurks. Fears are real. It can be nasty out there. But anglers always weigh the risks against the rewards. And so we go back to the water again and again.

CHAPTER 32

That Erie feeling

Here we are in Chapter 32 and I feel it is time you learn about a very real affliction that prevents me from seeking fulfillment of some of my biggest fishing dreams.

I get seasick.

There, I said it. It's an awful truth about me, the guy whose love of fishing and being out on the water helps define him. Many friends refer to me as The Fisherman. But I could justifiably be dubbed The Puker.

In my childhood days, Mom and Dad planned car trips that included frequent stops. Thirty minutes into a journey were enough to get me gagging in the back seat. My sister Kitty was, even at the tender age of four, horrified about the inevitable mess she would be sitting next to.

So Mom and Dad stopped the car twenty-nine minutes after leaving home and got me out to walk around to get my sea legs back under me. Then the trip would resume, the back seat was pristine, and Kitty could stop worrying about vomit in her lap.

Soon enough, as I grew taller and could see above the door windowsill of Dad's '57 Chevy, my motion sickness went into remission. I had no problem when I could keep visual contact with distant landscapes.

In 1976, Dad bought a Starcraft with a cuddy cabin and inboard in-line six-cylinder engine with a Mercruiser outdrive. It was a great boat for Lake Erie, where great schools of walleyes were eagerly gobbling Captain Dan Galbincea's famous Erie Dearies and other weight-forward spinners baited with night crawlers.

"Excited" barely describes the emotion bubbling in anglers when walleyes were on the comeback in Lake Erie in the mid-1970s. Highly prized as table fare, walleyes had dwindled as overfishing and pollution from ill-treated municipal sewage and industrial effluent put Erie on the brink of death. In 1972, Congress passed the Clean Water Act and new regulations took effect, resulting in cleaner water across the US, including Lake Erie. D'Arcy Egan of the *The Plain Dealer* in Cleveland and other outdoor writers began chronicling the return of the prized walleyes.

I guess you could say an act of Congress led to more walleyes in Erie, Dad buying a boat, and me relapsing into a life restrained by fear of motion sickness.

I was twenty-three, recently married to Barb, and jacked up about the prospects of joining the early fleet of anglers heading out to harvest our limits of Lake Erie walleyes. Dad, Barb, brother-in-law Gary Sipe, and I rode up to Erie and launched the boat on a sunny but blustery day. We probably should have kept the Starcraft on the trailer, but at twenty-one feet in length, it was enough boat to handle the waves.

Mark Franko rides Erie's waves without illness, but the author has been known to get seasick on the big lake.

That's what we thought. And it was, on paper anyway. Erie was rocking and rolling that morning. Nearby boats would disappear in the troughs of waves pushed along by the northwesterly wind. The Starcraft bobbed and bounced in sync with the rollers, and cresting whitecaps tossed a bit of spray as they slapped the gunwale.

It all seemed like a merry time to be on the water—for Barb and Dad. They decided it was time for sandwiches and Cokes. Gary and I were less enthusiastic. All that bobbing and bouncing was messing with our equilibrium. We tried to eat, but both lost the first bites of our lunches. Dad and Barb speculated maybe our chumming would help get the fish biting. Very funny.

If you've never been seasick, you probably have little sympathy for those who suffer the symptoms. And I do mean suffer. A victim might get a dry mouth, a dash of dizziness, and a queasy stomach. Sweat forms over the brow and around the hairline, and the head may ache. The victim fights to avoid vomiting, but it is inevitable. As a matter of fact, it often is welcome, as it seems to interrupt the cycle of nausea.

Medicines and spot-pressure application devices can forestall the onset of seasickness, but once it hits, the suffering is difficult to overcome. It has been said a person who is seasick fears he is going to die; then he fears he won't.

Lake Erie, among all the other superlatives it has earned, may also be the seasick capital of the world. I have been seasick on Erie more times than I can count. And yet I return again and again. I was seasick in my Arrowglass and my Ranger. I have been seasick aboard friends' boats and I've been seasick in my Bass Cat.

The funny thing about seasickness is that though the sufferer dreads the ailment, the reward seems to outweigh the risk. Going to puke? No big deal. Those smallmouth bass out there are huge.

Recently I ventured out on Erie in search of the five-pound smallies for which the lake is famous. Soon after setting up a drift over a spot I knew might attract a bite on my drop-shot setup rigged with a soft plastic goby bait, I felt the line tighten and twitch. I pulled back, and the circle-style hook grabbed the inside meat of the fish's upper lip. The fight was on, as the fish jumped several times and bulldogged at the side of the boat, as smallmouth are known to do. The encounter lasted only a minute or two, but it was long enough for me to lose my bearings relative to the horizon. By the time I had boated and unhooked the fish—a well-muscled and bulging-belly specimen weighing four pounds, fifteen ounces—my stomach was churning and sweat had soaked the band of my hat.

I tossed my cookies, as they say. Unable to will myself to relief, I fired up the engine and drove back to the shelter of the harbor, where within minutes I felt great. My first thought? Gotta get back out there for another go at those smallmouths.

I do confess, however, that I have passed on opportunities to venture far from port for an ocean adventure with marlin, yellowfin tuna, mahi-mahi, and other prized game species.

My bucket list will probably never show a check next to "Gulf Stream Charter," because I fear no dose of Dramamine is enough to KO the sickness induced by the swells of the bounding main.

That's my kryptonite, my Erie feeling.

CHAPTER 33

A spectacularly disappointing three seconds

I have never formally studied the matter, but I would venture a guess that for many anglers the span of time between our realization that we have hooked a big fish and the first opportunity to believe we are going to actually catch it is just a matter of seconds.

Much can happen in mere seconds out on the lake. An osprey dives. A beaver kerplunks its tail. A Jet Ski whizzes too close. A school of bait flitters. Anything and everything we might know or never imagine can happen in the wink of an eye on the water.

Anglers know this fact very well. Our fishing lives are defined as long periods of nothing interrupted by moments of exhilaration. The uninitiated might think those long periods are boring. Anglers know they are not. They do, as a matter of fact, add up as the time we invest in the activity of fishing. So it stands to reason that our experience on the water really is long periods of fishing interrupted by moments of catching.

I love those periods of fishing. They are where the real work happens. They are where the angler thinks, decides, and acts. They make all the difference in whether the moments of exhilaration will actually happen.

Sometimes the catching part is elusive. Catching can fail for a myriad of reasons. The angler might make bad decisions or execute sloppily enough that even a creature with a brain the size of your fingernail knows not to be fooled. Catching also can fail because of mechanical breakdowns. The line may break, a hook may straighten, or a reel can seize.

It's all part of fishing. When everything—literally everything—goes right, the angler will realize complete success. If you think that sounds like the odds are stacked against us, you are right. It's a miracle we catch as many fish as we do.

Consider, please, another element in the periodic table of the angling experience. Luck. Its atomic weight is inestimable. Some say it's not a matter of luck when anglers succeed; they say that intent combined with preparation and execution determines outcome. Yes, it does, but sometimes luck also intervenes.

I have never been one to discount luck in my own fishing, but I also hadn't put it front and center in my thoughts until recently, when I hooked and lost a big smallmouth bass. It was a particularly troubling experience. My disappointment lingered long after the boat was back at home in the garage. I recounted the moment and sad outcome in a text message to a friend and finished my description with the words "a spectacularly disappointing three seconds."

Three seconds was the time from the bite and hookset to the fish's showery aerial escape. I felt the tap of the smallie mouthing the bait, jerked to secure a connection, and held on as the fish surged with unbelievable power. Then it jumped to reveal its full-grown proportions—big head, broad body, and tail wide like a broom. In silhouette against the glare of the water, the fish's image etched firmly in my mind.

I remind you all of this transpired over a span of three seconds. Three seconds out of the 28,800 seconds I fished that day, but three seconds that burned far more intensely than the other 28,797. The three seconds started with anticipation (what had bit my bait?), switched to excitement (thrilled to have this fish on my line), and concluded in utter disappointment (what the hell just happened?).

In reflecting over that moment, and sharing it with you, I came to realize that the few-second sequence is not at all uncommon. Sometimes it's three seconds, sometimes it's five. But always there is that brief period of time when we finally get the bite we've been seeking and we light the fuse that will either fizzle to a dud or burst into sensational awesomeness.

Not to dwell on the negative, but the spectacularly disappointing three seconds—the duds—often are memorable. They teach us what not to do next time. They motivate us to get back on the horse and erase the ache. They show us the potential that awaits when we do eventually put it all together.

In the short span of seconds, the angler sets a chain of actions and reactions in motion. Often the outcome is that the fish is caught. Sometimes it is that the fish escapes. The savvy angler learns from both experiences and builds to be better when opportunity next bites.

CHAPTER 34

Ouch. That's going to hurt.

A surgeon in Canton, Ohio, earned enough money from operating on my body to pay for a year of college for one of his children. Thanks at least in part to the aggressive cast-and-retrieve style of fishing that I love, I wore out two thumb-wrist, carpometacarpal joints. Thank goodness we don't have more hands or it might have been three.

We fishers fully recognize ours is not a contact sport. Most injuries, therefore, are self-inflicted. I find it kind of appropriate that self-inflicted suffering is an outcome not just to our flesh and bones, but also to our psyche.

A baseball player is considered a failure if he or she gets a hit just every fifth at bat or so. A basketball player likely will never see the big time if only one out of every two foul shots falls through the net. A quarterback who connects on just a third of his passes will soon be asked to play wide receiver.

If only we anglers batted .200 on our fishing trips.

The muskie is considered the fish of a thousand casts. That would calculate to a batting average of .001.

I have actually counted my casts during bass fishing trips. Depending on what kind of lure or tactic I'm employing, I might make five or more casts per minute. I typically fish without much in the way of break time and I rarely sit while fishing, so it's reasonable to estimate I average eight hours of standing and casting while out on the boat chasing bass.

Figure I catch ten bass while making on average five casts per minute.

That's ten successes out of 2,400 attempts. Batting average: .004. Send me to the minor leagues!

But the reality is that .004 average, as measly as it is, can be worse. Much worse. It's failure magnified. Failure times one hundred compared with other endeavors in our lives. Imagine if we succeeded just .004 percent of the time at work. Hello, unemployment.

I usually am happy with a ten-fish day on the lake. Even five fish may be a good day, depending on the circumstances. But then there are the bad days. They can reduce an angler to a muttering shadow. They drag me down, for sure, and inflict the kind of pain that makes me wonder whether I've somehow lost the ability to trick those wild animals with brains the size of my thumbnail.

Psychological scars are common in the fishing community. Fishless days send anglers scurrying for excuses when friends ask about their luck. Broken lines and spit hooks leave fishers furious at their bad fortune. In my own case, I've flinched at the mental sting of explaining to Barb why I bothered to extend my full day on the lake when it was obvious the fish weren't cooperating.

Left: An angler's face sometimes gets in the path of flying lures. Right: Worn by many hundreds of thousands of casts, the carpometacarpal joints in both of the author's hands required surgical rebuilding.

The utter futility of failed fishing trips can pile on for those who find success to be elusive.

Some anglers who make their living at fishing hire coaches and psychologists to help them through the rough spots. They need mental fortitude to forge ahead on those days when their bank accounts are shrinking while their doubts are growing.

He or she who fishes who denies ever wondering "Why am I doing this?" is lying. Fishing can hurt us between the ears.

It also can hurt our muscles, our skin, and even our bones. Odds are if you fish as often as I've fished in my life, you will visit a doctor to fix something that happened as a result of the sun, the water, or the sheer repetitive nature of the mechanics that are necessary to put a lure in front of a fish.

Some of our injuries are accidental. A misstep can result in a fall that breaks a bone, tears a muscle, or twists a tendon or ligament. A flying hook can lodge in our skin. Sadly, a friend lost an eye to a spinner that flew back at bullet speed after dislodging from a snag.

Accidents happen. So do the self-inflicted injuries. The orthopedic surgeon who rebuilt my thumbs—both of them—explained that the 2,400 casts I've averaged during each of the thousands of days I've invested on the water were the main reason the vestigial trapezium bone wore away the cartilage in the carpometacarpal joint on both of my hands.

The damage was done thanks to the repetition of casting long rods that loaded up on each backcast and snapped forward to send lures flying to the fish I hoped were waiting. Do that enough times and it's certain to wear out a joint, just as surely as a bushing will wear out on a machine that works too hard for too long.

It was nothing that an hour under the knife and twelve weeks of rehab couldn't fix. I had a choice. I could choose to forgo the surgery and back away from fishing the way I love to fish. I chose instead to endure the surgery and rehab, twice in fact.

For many of us, almost no cost is too high to keep us from fishing. We may bat only a meager .004 on the lake and may return home sunburned and beaten. But we fish nevertheless. It's our passion.

CHAPTER 35

When it hurts, go fishing

Life is not without its ups and downs, so it is fortunate that we find ways to keep things in perspective.

We all have our own ways to cope. Some of them are good, some not so good. When life serves up lemons, some scowl about the sour hand they are dealt. Others reach for the sugar and make lemonade.

Fishing is my lemonade.

Call it an escape, a distraction, or a shield. Or call it a salve or a potion. Call it whatever you want, fishing is good medicine for me. Fishing softens the rough spots when life takes an unwelcome twist or turn.

For me in recent years, fishing is not about putting meat on the table. I may take a fish or two home from time to time, but the reality is that I prefer fishing for its therapeutic value.

Fishing helped pull me back into action following a heart attack in 2011. Fishing for a few hours, just me alone on the lake, helped me gain a bit of understanding after my mother passed away. It also helped fill the hole in my soul after Barb's father died. Fishing time and again has been helpful in bringing perspective when life has become complicated.

It may also have helped a friend take another step closer to the day when his doctor gives him the "all clear" sign. A day on the water is an escape, a distraction from concerns that can pile impossibly high if left as our sole focal point. During our time on the water, my friend and I talked little about our worries. No time for that. Our hours were about fish and habitat, lures and presentations, impressive topwater strikes and bulldogging bass. You know . . . important stuff.

We spotted a bald eagle in a tree and a deer on the bank. We swapped tales about past fishing adventures and commented on the changing season. Along the way, we caught a dozen bass between us, including a couple that would make any angler anywhere pretty darn proud.

It all was good. For five hours, it was something other than the loss of a loved one. It was time for cancer to take the back seat so that fishing could ride up front.

As all fishing trips do, ours came to an end. I loaded the boat on the trailer and stowed my rods. My friend hopped into his truck, and off we went in our separate directions, back to the other stuff that requires our attention.

But for that brief morning on the lake, we were not mourning and there were no illnesses on our minds.

Just two guys who love fishing, together on a boat with a common mission and nothing but the kind of optimism all anglers are known to exude.

Life will toss lemons. But as long as I've got fishing tackle and a way to get to the water, I've got the sweetest lemonade imaginable.

A day of fishing can be just the ticket to put worries in perspective.

CHAPTER 36

'Interesting' is not a euphemism

Here is a fish story with a little different angle.

For thirty-two years, most of the stories I have shared in my newspaper column have been woven with the thread of fishing success. Considering that history, some readers may have believed we always filled the boat with fish.

That was not the case. We returned home some days with nothing to show for our efforts.

This is a story about one of those days. The weather forecast was great. After a couple days of rain and small-craft warnings, Lake Erie was to lay down. The steelhead had been hitting, and I was jazzed about the prospects of trolling the breakwater around Conneaut Harbor on Lake Erie.

Fishing friend Ted Suffolk took the bait when I offered him a seat. Ted likes two of the things I like: fishing and golfing. When we get together, the conversation always drifts to those topics.

Ted was assistant general manager of *The Vindicator* in Youngstown, Ohio, which published my column for thirty-one years before it closed in 2019. That's not the reason I invited him on fishing trips, but I figured it's good form to deliver for one of the bosses.

It is a good thing Ted is a good-natured fellow. Based on our performance that day, he might have started lobbying to fire me.

For reasons I cannot fully comprehend, the fishing fizzled. There are many ways to measure a fishing trip's success, but if the main thing is catching fish, our outing was a flop.

Ted, to his credit, didn't exactly see it that way.

"It was a very interesting day," he said as I wiped down the boat in the launch parking lot. "I've never fished out of Conneaut, and learned a lot about the water."

Interesting? Ted didn't mean it as a euphemism for disappointing, but I was pretty sour about our results.

Several years ago, I coaxed *Vindicator* editor Todd Franko to fish on a pro-am team for the annual Muransky Companies Bass Classic. It's a fundraiser for the United Way of Youngstown and the Mahoning Valley, and Todd graciously agreed to fish second seat with one of the pros.

Seven hours on a boat is a long time, especially for a man busy with kids and managing a daily paper's newsroom. I know Todd would have rather been golfing that Saturday morning instead of greeting his pro at 5:30 in the chill fog. But he acknowledged his fishing experience had been "interesting."

Fast-forward to the day Ted and I shared. He managed to hook one of Lake Erie's prized steelhead trout. His rod bucked vigorously as the fish surged, and then the line went slack.

"It's gone," Ted said matter-of-factly.

I was more disappointed than Ted. He probably was hedging his feelings based on the optimism he gained while listening to my recounting of my previous steelhead trip—and the thirty fish we caught.

Fishers are by nature optimistic. Lose a fish? Another will come soon. Haven't had a bite in a couple of hours? The next cast may produce.

I figured we'd get more—many more—hookups that day. But after several hours of trolling spoons and plugs without a strike, we came to doubt we had made the right decision.

"We should have gone golfing," I said. Ted smiled. He probably agreed, but he insisted he'd found our day to be "interesting."

"We'll get them next time." Ever the optimists.

CHAPTER 37

To stink or not to stink

Many years ago, too many to count, friend Bob warned us to avoid eating garlic the day before a bass tournament.

He reasoned that the odor that escapes through our pores the morning after a garlicky meal would transfer to our fishing lures and repel the bass we were trying to catch.

Bob swore it was fact. It seemed to make sense. Many of us believed him and for years avoided spaghetti dinners on the eve of fishing trips.

And then along came commercial garlic-scented fish attractant we anglers bought to spray directly on our lures—on purpose!

Today the shelves of your favorite fishing tackle store are stocked with all kinds of potions and dyes to customize our lures. Always on the alert for tricks that may turn the tables in their favor, anglers experiment in changing the ways their lures present compared with the hundreds of others a fish might see during the fishing season.

The two more obvious tricks are color and smell.

Anglers can tinker with their lures to make them stand apart. We add a splash of color to create an illusion that our target species perceives as interesting or tasty or even menacing in a manner that provokes an attack.

The most popular lure dyes are chartreuse, orange, and red.

When the mood strikes me, I'll pull out a dye marker and dab a dot of color on a bait's belly or slash a streak across its flank. On crawfish-imitating baits' pinchers, I'll pull the pen down the length to add a provocative flair.

The extra attention seems to pay dividends. I say "seems" because I have no hard numbers as proof that I get more bites when I doctor my lures, but I believe it helps.

Believing is one of the most important factors in fishing. If you believe you will fool a fish, you are more likely to succeed than if you cast with doubts. Belief builds confidence, and confidence helps us focus. When we are riveted in every aspect of our fishing, we cast more accurately, fish more intentionally, and react with more assertiveness.

So a splash of color to differentiate a bait is worth it to me.

The same goes for adding scent. Fish hunt with all of their senses, and while some fish are more reliant on their sense of smell than others, all of them rely to some extent on sniffing out their prey.

Steve Zarbaugh tricked a bass by differentiating his lure from those the fish might typically encounter.

It would seem wise then to douse our baits with the scent of shad or crawfish, two of the main food sources for game fish in most fresh water. But what about garlic and other offbeat scents, like anise, blueberry, and even WD-40, the penetrating oil found in just about every garage and workshop in America?

Some say the food-like smells—and the oddball scents too—work to mask the human odor we add to lures as we handle them during our fishing trips. So if a largemouth bass is reluctant to investigate a bait that smells like people, would that fish throw caution to the wind when that same bait smells like a plate of Italian greens and beans?

That question may go forever unanswered. But the reason does not matter as much as the result.

Results are what we want. If we think it matters that our bait smells like a big crawfish, with a splash of orange on its back and streaks of chartreuse on its pinchers, then that's what we'll throw.

I have a marker that does all of that. I can customize my baits' colors and scents with that single tool with confidence.

When I'm confident, I fish better, and the results pile up naturally.

CHAPTER 38

Alligators and bouncing bobbers

Two friends from Youngstown, Ohio, met for lunch at a spot south of Fort Myers, Florida, and soon enough the conversation drifted to fishing.

The waiter took their order and left for the kitchen, leaving the friends to catch up on what had been happening since they last spoke face-to-face months ago back home in Youngstown.

One of them mentioned he golfs twice a week and fishes two other days a week during his extended stay in Southwest Florida. The other said his schedule is pretty similar.

"You know, it's different here than around Youngstown," said one. "Here we need to look out for things like alligators."

Indeed. Phil Dennison is right about that.

Best known around Youngstown as one of the bosses at a big, busy accounting and consulting firm and for his involvement in numerous civic activities, Phil also is an avid angler.

He loves fishing waters near his winter residence in Florida and his summer home in Ohio. His fishing passion also has taken him to Alaska to cast for salmon.

Our lunchtime conversation ebbed and flowed around business, real estate values, healthy eating, the fun and frustrations of golf, and eventually fishing. Not the existential kind of fishing talk—why we fish and what it all means—but rather the simple pragmatics.

"A fellow who lives nearby saw me fishing in one of our community's ponds. He said, 'You better be careful. Watch out for alligators,'" Phil said. "Turns out the guy once was unhooking a bass while holding it in the water right at his feet, and whoosh! An alligator grabbed the fish while it was still hooked."

We both laughed. In Florida, you can catch more than you bargained for.

On the water, we never know when trouble may strike. Years ago, Phil joined me for a day on the Ohio River with our mutual friend Rich Pisani. Phil hooked and landed a spunky river bass that thrashed while he was trying to unhook it.

Unfortunately, one of the treble hooks on the lure dug into his thumb. It looked pretty nasty, and I turned to fetch pliers and an alcohol swab.

Watch out for gators!

Before I returned, however, he'd jerked the hook out by himself and was ready to resume fishing.

I suppose a hook in the hand is less of a problem than some of the pickles he had to cure in his long career as a CPA and business adviser. These days, his work is such that he's able to retreat to warm weather while Youngstown shivers under snow and ice.

As it does for many, fishing helps Phil keep things in perspective. He enjoys casting to largemouth bass, but also gets a special kick out of catching the cichlids in the shallows of ponds near his house.

"I love bass fishing with lures, but there's something intriguing about watching the bobber bounce as panfish bite. I can do that all day and it's still fun," Phil said.

His rig is simple: a tiny hook baited with a bit of hot dog hanging under a small float. It reminded me of days long ago when I could pass an entire afternoon catching chubs in Yellow Creek with a bit of worm on a tiny hook hanging under a small float.

The fun thing about fishing is it doesn't have to be complicated. It's whatever we want it to be wherever we are in life.

But remember to watch out for the gators.

CHAPTER 39
That's Hollywood

Screenwriters and playwrights are pretty good about capturing the essence of characters and situations in scripts that result in very real portrayals and believable stories. It is important, of course, that they get it right, because their audience will buy what they are selling only if it is credible. If it doesn't pass the sniff test, people will label it BS.

Hollywood gets it right when scripting cops and criminals, lawyers and doctors, teachers and coaches, moms and dads, and just about every other character.

And then there is fishing. It cracks me up that TV and movies often fail in depicting the world of fishing.

Some get it right. *A River Runs Through It*, for example, does an excellent job in portraying the art, science, and appeal of fly fishing for trout. Two brothers, portrayed by Brad Pitt and Craig Sheffer, fish their way to maturity in a riveting story made believable thanks in part to the well-done fishing scenes.

Grumpy Old Men also worked for me, but I'm not sure it wasn't more a case of perfect chemistry between actors Jack Lemmon and Walter Matthau than great depictions of fishing action. The characters' funky hats and fishing clothes play to stereotypical notions about anglers' attire, and some scenes teeter on the edge of exaggeration. Nevertheless, it's a movie that puts fishing in a believable perspective.

Jaws and *The Old Man and the Sea* are two classics that dramatized the allure of the water and the driven nature of people who fish against all odds. *On Golden Pond* is another acclaimed film about a man and his quest for the fish of a lifetime. Henry Fonda's character would never be satisfied until "Walter" was in his boat.

For all that they achieve, however, *A River Runs Through It*, *Grumpy Old Men*, and *On Golden Pond* are not enough to persuade me that all of the motion picture and television industry understands fishing.

Take hats, for instance. It seems as though every director and costume designer thinks they add authenticity when they put a porkpie hat and sleeveless vest on their fisherman characters. I have fished for more than fifty years and never encountered an angler with a misshapen hat festooned with spinners, plugs, flies, and whatnot. I can understand the amplification of angler stereotypes like those in Carl Hiaasen's spoofy *Double Whammy*, but not when believability is based on reality.

So let's get real. I have seen lots of anglers dressed like Andy Griffith as Sheriff Taylor and Ron Howard as Opie as they ambled with fishing rods in hand through the opening segment of the 1960s TV series *The Andy Griffith Show*.

Andy and Opie made me believe they were going to their lake somewhere near Mayberry, North Carolina, with the not-a-care-in-the-world attitude all anglers seek to achieve.

Truth is, not many TV shows even try to make fishing part of the storyline. That's probably a good thing, because those that do apparently think it unnecessary to hire a real angler as an authenticity consultant.

I loved the long-running TV mockumentary *Modern Family*. Each episode, while obviously leaning on opportunities to emphasize eccentricities, helped me appreciate the realities in our society as we struggle with pride and prejudice, dreams and dramas, obstacles and opportunities, and everything else that makes modern living what it is.

I laughed heartily during each episode and marveled at the producers' and directors' keen depictions of the situations the cast of characters worked through week in and week out. I may have thought Phil Dunphy sometimes a bit too bouncy or Haley a little too ditzy, but I bought in weekly.

Then they sent Jay Pritchett fishing. OK, sure, lots of self-made millionaires with trophy wives and fancy automobiles go fishing. But the director goofed. They put the spinning reel in Jay's hands upside down.

It was one scene in a series that featured thousands of scenes, but they blew it.

I knew immediately Jay was not a fisherman. I wanted to believe the character played by actor Ed O'Neill, who grew up in my hometown, played football for my alma mater, Youngstown State University, and worked out at the club where I played racquetball. I wanted to believe Jay Pritchett was enjoying fishing the way I enjoy fishing.

But that upside-down spinning reel told me he was just going through the motions.

This meme says it all when Hollywood goofs up in representing fishing. The downside-up spinning reel sends a clear message that the person responsible for that image has no clue about for-real fishing.

CHAPTER 40
The angler's obligation

In a world where environmental catastrophes happen all too often, it would be easy to dismiss as insignificant the footprints we anglers leave every time we go to the water.

Our footprint is not just the mark in the mud or snow. The gasoline we burn, the litter we leave, the fish we harvest, the lures we lose, and probably a dozen other deeds we do are footprints every bit as real as the imprint of our shoes in the earth below our feet.

They pile up to affect our air and water and our flora and fauna. Eventually, our footprints will obscure the beauty and bounty.

So what's an angler to do? How do we avoid trampling the environment?

We begin by paying attention to details—the big things and the little. It may not seem significant if your sandwich wrapper blows into the lake, but can you imagine if everyone on the water that day let their paper fly?

What do you do with your soda cans, water bottles, chip bags, and bait containers? Judging by the trash I see on local causeways, I'd say lots of people are OK with just leaving that stuff on the bank.

If you smoke, do you toss the butts in the lake? When you blow your nose, does the tissue go in your pocket or ride the wind?

Sometimes, litterbugs aren't deliberate. They aren't necessarily bad people who care not about the next angler to visit the lake. Many, I suspect, simply are not aware of the damage they are doing.

Consider the boater who goes to the lake with an outboard motor that needs a tune-up. Who cares, right? It's no big deal if the motor is spewing blue smoke and spitting unburned fuel out the exhaust port, is it?

Tell that to the fish that swim in your lake and the people who drink that water. Ask them if they are OK with you lugging out the Evinrude your grandfather bought in 1958.

Have you ever caught a fish and discovered it was gut-hooked? Did you carefully extract the hook or snip the line to free the fish? Or did you yank the hook and pull the fish's stomach into its throat?

How many of us have released a mortally wounded fish when the right thing to do would have been to make sure someone made it into a meal?

Conservationists counsel us to reduce, reuse, and recycle.

Have you ever kept more fish than your legal limit? Those who do are leaving too big of a footprint.

Have you ever tossed a pop can in the barrel at the launch ramp instead of taking it home to your recycling bin? You have a recycling bin at home, right?

Have you discarded a perfectly usable plastic worm in favor of a fresh bait? We all are tempted by the seemingly endless supply that a one

Anglers are encouraged to recycle or properly dispose of used plastic baits.

hundred pack of plastics promises.

Here's a bad thing I used to do: I would toss a torn plastic bait into the lake instead of stashing it in the boat for proper disposal at home. Tattered plastics can be melted and re-formed.

And what happens to all of that fishing line we replace each year? I consume no fewer than a thousand yards a year myself. Tens of thousands of miles of anglers' used line end up in landfills and—worse—streams, lakes, and trails, where birds, mammals, fish, and reptiles get tangled, maimed, and killed.

Those are mighty big feet we take to the water. But by being aware and doing what is right, we can do something to keep from trampling our planet.

Two large ziplock bags on the bench in my fishing shop look harmless enough, but their contents pack the potential for a nasty ecological punch.

One bag stores monofilament and fluorocarbon fishing line replaced over the past season. The other is full of tattered soft plastic worms and creature baits.

Fortunately, where I do much of my fishing we have opportunities to make sure our old fishing line and unusable plastic worms won't contribute to environmental nightmares.

The local county Green Team, in cooperation with the US Army Corps of Engineers, promotes fishing line reclamation and recycling stations. Anglers can drop off mono and fluorocarbon lines at any of ten locations near two busy local lakes.

Want to recycle your old soft plastics? Find a person who collects worn baits, melts them, and pours new baits. If you cannot locate such a resource, at least make sure they are properly disposed of and not left to fester in the wild, where animals might ingest them.

Fishing line is a major headache around lakes and rivers and out in the wide-open ocean. If discarded improperly, it can foul habitat and ensnare everything that walks, wiggles, slinks, swims, or flies close to its loops and tangles.

Plastic worms are trouble too. They take years to break down and can find their way into the digestive systems of reptiles, amphibians, fish, waterfowl, and mammals, where they are virtually indigestible. They can swell up in guts and cause distress and death.

We anglers owe it to our fish and other wildlife to make sure the line we replace and the plastics we use aren't left to do harm.

The stuff stashed in those two ziplocks in my shop packs enough wallop to be disastrous. One bag has close to nine thousand yards of old line. That's twenty-seven thousand feet, more than five miles. Imagine the giant snare it could become if discarded recklessly.

I'm just one angler. Millions of anglers replace their fishing lines; many do it multiple times each year. It would be reasonable to guess that just in my corner of Ohio we replace enough line to crisscross the US three times or more.

I encourage all anglers to save the line they replace next time they respool along with their no-longer-usable plastic grubs, twisters, worms, craws, swimbaits, and trailers. Bag them up and dispose of them properly, recycling them if possible. In fact, fishing product marketer Strike King includes in each package of fishing line a postage-paid addressed envelope to return the old line for recycling.

Reduce, reuse, and recycle. It's not always convenient. I know that. But it's the right thing to do. I know that too.

Three simple words: Reduce. Reuse. Recycle.

CHAPTER 41

Red tide and caring voices

Sometimes, the irony is unreal.

As has come to be common behavior for many of us, I was scanning my phone during an idle moment. Go figure. The beautiful and lightly peopled beach and the rolling waters apparently were not enough to occupy my senses. So I idly scrolled through the messages on the screen, a task made all the more difficult by peering through the polarized lenses of my sunglasses.

The beach is a place where one should not be distracted by the worries of the world. The warm sand, ever-changing waves, and limitless horizon are salve for our wounds, good hope in trying times, and pleasure for our human senses. The beach is hardly the place where one needs wireless stimulation.

Nonetheless, I looked. But I couldn't believe my eyes. The word "hiatus" stuck out like a sore thumb. What?

It was an email from the editor of the newspaper that published my column. The email informed me and others about a decision to slim down the newspaper. The weekly outdoors page was eliminated, and thus the fishing column I'd written weekly for thirty years was on hiatus. After more than fifteen hundred columns, I had lost—at least temporarily—the honor of entertaining and informing readers.

It was a gut punch. People endure news far more devastating than what I'd just read, but that didn't make the message any easier to process.

My column had evaporated, like a drop of water on a hot sidewalk.

What?

Barb was sitting two feet away, enjoying the same beach and ocean view from which I'd been distracted. We were in South Florida, far from the bleak winter at home in Ohio. I told her what I'd learned.

What?

It wasn't the money. I was paid just a tad north of what a volunteer would be paid, so it factored little in our lifestyle—other than that I had to let the IRS know about it every year.

As we discussed the matter, the irony began to hit me. The newspaper was on a weight-reduction program, but it was cutting muscle instead of fat. I do not say this as a matter of braggadocio. I began my professional career as a news reporter. I fully embrace the importance of the news media in informing the electorate and protecting life and liberty from those who would take it away. I understand the first duty of the media is to learn the news and inform their audiences, followed closely by the duty to earn enough money to sustain the resources that enable reporters, photographers, editors, printers, drivers, and all the others to do their jobs properly.

They, indeed, are the muscle. We need strong journalists to fulfill their employers' editorial obligations. As the paper's fishing writer, I saw myself as one fiber of that muscle. Yes, I wrote about topics that hardly matter as our world tumbles through time and space, but I also provided a little more perspective on matters important to my readers and a distraction from the evils and sadness created by those who believe it is their way or the highway.

I glanced out at the beach and Gulf of Mexico. I saw no diving birds. A couple of stiff mullet washed up on the sand. A whiff of red tide reached my nostrils.

The irony overwhelmed me.

Somewhere not far from my chair on the beach, pollution trickled into a creek. As the runoff drained toward the Gulf of Mexico, it was fortified by the effluent from dozens more creeks that also were fouled with nutrients that enable certain microorganisms to thrive. Gravity pulls the creeks' currents to rivers and bays, and the polluted water soon feeds so many bacteria that they bloom into toxic populations known as red tide.

People create red tide. People can reduce red tide. But people need to know about red tide before they can care about it.

A few will see the dearth of diving birds and the rafts of stiff mullet and dead dolphins washing up on the beach. Eyewitnesses will be outraged by the consequences of red tide, but relatively powerless to enact change that stops the fouling of waterways.

Red tide is but one of a myriad of environmental calamities that threaten our planet. Overfertilized water draining to Lake Erie from important agricultural lands is blamed for annual blooms of toxic blue-green algae across thousands of acres of the lake's western basin. It stinks, for sure, but it also kills fish.

The fish aren't the only victims of the dirt we produce. Polluted water and air make people sick and cause many to die. Despite such dire outcomes, many would look the other way when it comes to preventive measures.

Ospreys, manatees, and all the other life on Earth depend on clean water and anglers' stewardship.

People who care about red tide, blue-green algae blooms, and all the other problems that can prove toxic for life on Earth need a voice. News reporters help in that regard. As do fishing columnists and all the others who have opportunities to spread the word about threats to our environment. People need to be heard, and they need to be informed. We see, we share, and we issue calls to action.

Fishers, hunters, kayakers, sailors, surfers, beach bums, conservationists, and many other interests compose a significant percentage of the voice for our planet's care. Their voices are amplified by scientists and activists far and wide.

Without such voices, our Earth will someday morph into a shriveled cinder spinning pointlessly around the sun, its ability to sustain life snuffed not just until the red tide turns or the algae blooms fade, but forever.

I saw the effects of red tide on the day I learned my newspaper put my column on hiatus. My weekly six hundred words were but a fraction of the voice that unites those who fish, but a voice nonetheless. The column provided information and amusement for readers and for me.

The irony of the day, however, was more than a column put on hiatus. As the red tide rolled, I was reminded that fishing, for many, provides perspective, distraction, and even purpose.

So it is for such reasons that we fish. And write, paint, cook, carve, work, play, and live. Do what you love, with all of your heart, mind, and soul. Your passion may not be my passion, but it will make you a better person. Our world needs more people like us.

The tide will turn. It can happen. I know this. The red tide dissipated. The fish and birds returned to the beach. And after a two-week hiatus, the paper brought back my column.

Many things can be learned from fishing, like not having to take things the way they are. We learn if we want a different outcome, we need to change our tactics. But we also know there are times when we must persevere, to forge ahead with the confidence we are doing the right things.

Funny how much we can learn if we just pay attention.

FINAL WORDS:

Where we've been and where we're going

As sure as the fish are biting somewhere, we will continue to go to the water with a curiosity, a goal, and a plan.

I am among those who believe our existence is not so much a matter of what happens to us as we bump along, but rather how we toil to put ourselves in positions of opportunity. What do we see? What do we learn? How do we adjust? We can control where we are in our lives and where we are going. And when I go fishing, I can control where I am and decide where I wish to go next.

Along the way, of course, things change. Lessons are learned, love blooms, accidents happen, illness strikes—and when they do, we work things out, just as we do on the water when weather and a myriad of other factors come and go as our day moves and time ticks.

Yes, I have a special passion for fishing. I am a common angler who has attempted in the preceding chapters to unravel, understand, and share the real meaning, the special joy, that my body and soul associate with fishing. I believe I have come close to that goal, but the truth is I have learned it is impossible. Words cannot adequately express the moments, especially those we experience when we really stop, look, and listen to all the signs around us.

Next time you go to the water, open your eyes wider than ever before. Listen like your ears are amplifiers. Breathe with a purpose, deep and slow, so every molecule of nature checks in with your brain. Feel the sun.

Touch the water. Ask yourself why you are there and what you intend to accomplish.

Do this and you will be fishing. Do it every time and you will open a new chapter in your life as an angler.

Just as life is a journey with countless waypoints and an ever-changing destination, fishing is a journey. Our trips to the water begin and end, but the act of angling really is infinite. Anglers can say where we have been. We can say where we are going. But we cannot know where we will end up, because there always will be more lakes to explore, more casts to make, and more fish to catch.

Fishers are famous for stretching the day. An unfathomable number of fishing trips have started the countdown to conclusion with an angler declaring, "One more cast." Comrades chuckle; they know there will be at least another and probably even another after that. Eventually, the last cast is made, but it happens with the assurance that another trip is on the horizon.

We all know we will have a final fishing trip. We just hope it hasn't already happened. Right?

Passionate anglers go to the water with more than meat in mind. Their search is for more than a tug on a line. They go to gain understanding about their own instincts and skills. They go to satisfy an urge so primordial that it quite possibly is in our DNA. They go with a thirst for knowledge that cannot ever be completely quenched.

Every day for an angler starts with a clean slate and the opportunities of a lifetime. So can we ever be blamed for our passion for fishing? Every day since our very first encounter with a fish on a hook, we have been building the base for today and the springboard for tomorrow.

Make your next fishing trip the one that starts the best time of your life. Go with confidence and go again and again.

ACKNOWLEDGMENTS

I am supremely thankful to the following people for their contributions to *The Common Angler*:

Lee-Ann Mitchell DeMeo for her keen eye and deft touch on the covers of *The Common Angler*.

Diane Laney Fitzpatrick for counsel about the challenges of writing a book.

Donna Saber Nickel, Jim Cyphert, Jeff Rios, Dick Maggiore, Betsy Wollitz Khan, Jeannie Wollitz Tarka, and Kitty Sipe—all early content reviewers.

Bob and Dale Mullen for showing me the excitement around competitive bass fishing.

Harry Stewart for encouraging a young *Salem News* reporter to pitch an article to a local outdoors magazine. Woody Earnhart, Ottie Snyder, and Michael Hoffman for buying early manuscripts from a fledgling fishing writer.

Bob Cobb, Dave Precht, and Matt Vincent for entrusting me to write articles for *Bassmaster* and *Bass Times* and enabling me to get an insider's perspective on the world of professional fishing.

David Bushman for editing the book and Scott Ryan for the design.

David Lee Morgan, Jr., for introducing me to Fayetteville Mafia Press.

And finally, to each and every reader who has lent their precious time to read the tales I have written for them.

ABOUT THE AUTHOR

Jack Wollitz has been a passionate angler ever since he went on his first fishing trip at the age of five. He grew to love writing about fishing as much as actually fishing and has published more than two hundred magazine feature stories along with nearly 1,700 weekly columns in the *Youngstown Vindicator* and *Warren Tribune Chronicle*. After graduating with a bachelor of arts in English from Youngstown State University, he worked as a newspaper reporter for *The Salem News* in Ohio and then joined the editorial staff of the *Warren Tribune Chronicle*. He later worked in marketing and public relations for ad agencies, retiring in 2018 as director of public relations at positioning agency Innis Maggiore in Canton, Ohio. Jack and wife Barb reside in Poland, Ohio, and Naples, Florida, and are the parents of a daughter, Betsy Wollitz Khan, of Columbus, Ohio.

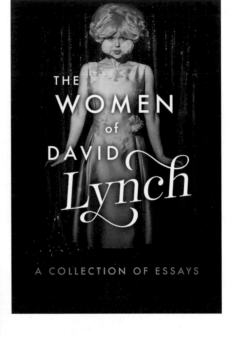
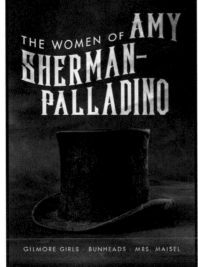

Moonlighting: An Oral History by Scott Ryan. Cybill Shepherd and Bruce Willis starred in one of the hottest shows in the eighties. Now the cast, writers and crew talk about how the series was made and what caused the show to end.

ISBN: 9781949024265

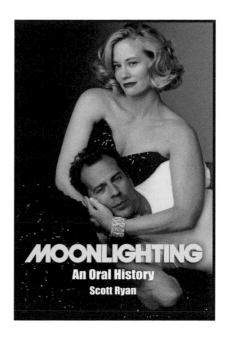

Scarlett Harris takes a deep dive into the world of female wrestling and some of the greatest characters in all of sports.

A Diva Was a Female Version of a Wrestler

ISBN: 9781949024180

KEN H. FORTENBERRY

FLIGHT 7

IS MISSING

THE SEARCH FOR MY FATHER'S KILLER

Ken Fortenberry solves one of the greatest real-life mysteries in aviation history as he searches for the killer of his father and the cause of the crash of Flight 7.

ISBN: 9781949024067

Laura's Ghost: Women Speak about Twin Peaks
by Courtenay Stallings with a foreword by Sheryl Lee.
Women discuss how Laura Palmer influenced their lives.

ISBN: 9781949024081

LAURA'S GHOST:
Women Speak about Twin Peaks

By Courtenay Stallings
Foreword by Sheryl Lee

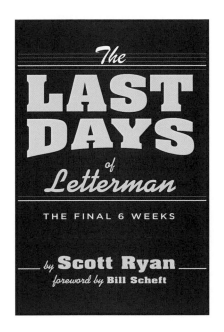

An inside look at the final six weeks of *Late Show with David Letterman,* all told through the words of the staff that wrote, directed, and produced those iconic last twenty-eight episodes in 2015. *The Last Days of Letterman* by Scott Ryan

ISBN: 9781949024005

Mark Frost cocreated *Twin Peaks*, wrote for *Hill Street Blues,* and has written over ten books. Learn about his life, his craft, and his career in this new book by David Bushman.

ISBN: 9781949024104

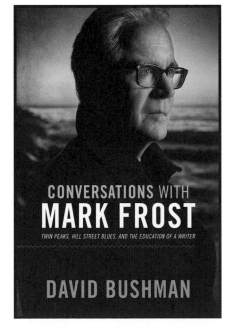

Cracking The Wire During Black Lives Matter
Edited by Ronda Racha Penrice

Essays by African American writers about the television series *The Wire*. Coming November 2021.

ISBN: 9781949024289

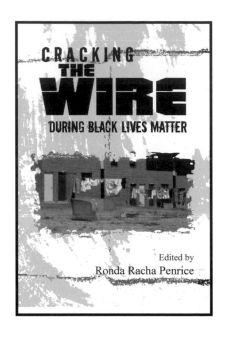

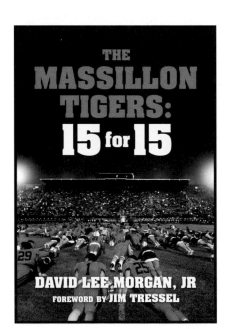

The Massillon Tigers: 15 for 15 by David Lee Morgan, Jr., with a foreword by Jim Tressel. Follow along with the Ohio high school football powerhouse team the Massillon Tigers as they hunt for a state championship in 2019.

ISBN: 9781949024166

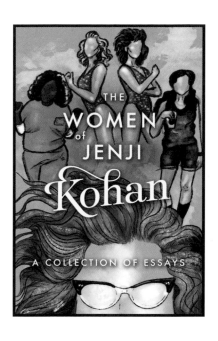

The Women of Jenji Kohan: Orange is the New Black, GLOW, and Weeds
Edited by Scarlett Harris

Essays about the female characters from Kohan's TV series. Coming April 2022.

ISBN: 9781949024302

Fire Walk With Me: Your Laura Disappeared
by Scott Ryan

A look at the 30th anniversary of David Lynch's *Twin Peaks* movie. Foreword by screenwriter Robert Engels. Coming Summer 2022.

ISBN: 9781949024241